It's Not about the Food:

Battling through your child's eating disorder

D1613016

Tracy Baines

It's Not About the Food:
Battling through your child's eating disorder

Published by The Meggie Press 2017
www.themeggiepress.co.uk

First Published 2017

ISBN 13: 978-0-9957423-0-7
ISBN 10: 0-9957423-0-8

For mothers and fathers everywhere

especially my own

Tom and Joan Lee

Contents

Part One   **A Mother's Story**

Introduction

Part Two   **Practicalities**

Part One

A Mother's Story

Introduction

I was her mother, I should've known – shouldn't I?
When I found out my daughter was suffering from an
eating disorder (and it is suffering) I was devastated.
Mostly I was terrified that we would lose her. Isn't that
every parent's worst fear? Losing their child? It was a
shock. I had thought eating disorders were all about
food but I was wrong. I had a lot to learn – as a family
we all did. We came through, eventually, but not
without it leaving its scars. I've wanted to write this
book for a long time but when you're in the middle of
the madness that accompanies an eating disorder, or
any mental health illness for that matter, it's hard to
step back and observe the pandemonium that you are
caught in. It took me a long time to be able to find my
bearings and search for a way out of it. But I did, and I
hope I can help you to do that too.

I finally understand that there are no quick fixes,
there are only possibilities. I'm not a medical
professional, counsellor or psychologist but I consider
myself a professional of sorts – a professional mother.
And I am an expert. And if you are the parent of a child
with an eating disorder so are you. You're there in the
field of battle, and believe me it's a daily battle, dealing
with the challenges, the highs and lows, the little
successes, the downright devastation of coping with
the situation. Yep, if you're not now you definitely will
become an expert. Frightening, isn't it? After six years
on the front line I feel qualified to share my story, our
story, in the hope that it helps someone else who may
be floundering about in the dark as I was. At this point
in my journey what I can offer is this: take comfort in

the fact that you are not alone, that you cannot solve all of the problems all of the time, that you can support your child but you cannot fix them – they have to do that for themselves – and you have to learn to let them, hard as it is. Letting go will revitalise you and give you the energy to cope with whatever comes your way.

I haven't written all the ins and outs of Nelly's illness, her time when she was deep in the grip of the eating disorder. This book was never about that. Other writers who personally suffered with an ED have told the nightmare of their journey and I could not possibly know what Nelly thought and felt during this time. Nor is this a book about the nitty-gritty of an eating disorder from a medical viewpoint. I have written about what it feels like to watch someone you love suffer from a mental illness. I have written from my own experience and I have written about my fear. A fear that I believe kept me disabled and unable to help her properly as well as nearly bringing myself to my knees.

My immediate reaction was that we needed to get her help, professional help; and, once we had her in the medical system, feeling somewhat supported I stumbled forward in a daily stupor. I recognise that look now on other parents' faces when they talk of their child's eating disorder, that hollow eyed fear that takes over. I've come to know that talking about our fears makes them smaller. To know that someone else has walked in your shoes and survived makes it a little easier to bear. It gives you hope, and hope is what we need in abundance if we are to support our child through these darkest of times. My daughter is well now, although I am vigilant to any stressors that might tip her into the abyss again.

Back then, I was desperate for information on how best to help her, how best to help myself. I felt an abject failure as a mother and an out and out fool as to why I hadn't noticed the signs. Therefore, to my mind, I was stupid as well as neglectful. Add on as many negative emotions as you can think of, believe me, I felt them all. Blame, blame and more blame. Not that anyone else uttered a word. But I knew. My family turned to me for how to react and I am grateful that through the worst of times we were a united front. Lots of things went unspoken but we were like a wall, a dam, keeping the storm water and tornados at bay – and my daughter knew that we wouldn't crack. I was determined that there was no way my family unit would be a casualty of the war that was going on inside my beautiful daughter – but it wasn't easy.

Most people think that eating disorders only affect the victim, the sufferer, but everyone in the family suffers. The shockwaves ripple on and on. What I had thought was real was not. It made me doubt my judgement, my parenting skills, my caring skills, my life choices. Even now, almost six years later, I am only beginning to realise how deeply it affected me – and still does to some extent. At last I am starting to make sense of it, more able to understand how it crept insidiously into our lives. I still get anxious, always on alert, always searching for someone else with the same story and how they coped (or didn't), sadly aware of how many of our beautiful children are hurting themselves in this way. Although eating disorders affect mainly girls, boys suffer too. Has it always been so? Or are the everyday pressures of society getting too much for our children to bear?

What I really wanted to know most of all was that there was someone else out there who felt as I did, who could tell me that I wasn't odd, or losing my grip on reality, that this would be my new normal. I suppose I was seeking a point of reference when my world was falling apart. Coming to the end of writing this book has made me realise I was looking for a book of answers, a book that would tell me exactly what to do so that I could solve my problem. I couldn't grasp that there were no concrete solutions, and that there was no 'way' I could follow that would make everything right.

The other experts in this book are parents/carers whose day to day is taken with caring for their child or partner, whose path is a delicate balance between providing sympathy and empathy, support, and a kick up the arse when needed. The challenge is to know when each situation requires which response. It is mentally draining and you need all the assistance and support you can get.

To get a range of points of view I developed a questionnaire which I sent out to parents via various resources and some of their responses are included in what follows. Other parents I met at support groups and other social occasions. Talking to parents in the same position was the first time I had felt at ease. I was completely free to say what I felt without having to consider responses and reactions. I always experienced myself as on the outside when in a medical/official situation. I thought that was just me being hypersensitive but since speaking to other parents I realise that many experienced the same.

I'm a great fan of keeping things simple. Life is

stressful enough without making it even more complicated. As such I wanted to keep this book simple. When I was in the middle of this mess I couldn't concentrate on reading large amounts of detailed text and I expect many of you will be the same. I'm not going to tell you in immense detail how to help your child get well. It would be impossible for a start because we are all individuals and so are our children. Our responses will be different according to our experience and personality and, as I have already discovered, there are no easy options, no clear answers to what you will experience as a parent or carer of someone suffering from an eating disorder. What I hope to do is share a little of my story and point you in the direction of some great resources that could support you if you should need it.

Chapter 1: Sanctuary

Sanctuary. The bathroom. The only room where I couldn't be 'got at', asked to do anything for anyone else. Although, I am aware that it made me a sitting target. I should have locked the door but that would be a step too far. Husband and daughter would come in, sit on a chair or loo seat to chat, son stood outside the closed door, asking questions, telling me in finite detail about his latest escapades.

Mostly I was left alone, bubbles, candles, soft music, tea ferried in at regular intervals. Sometimes I had lain there for an hour and a half, wrinkling away, uninterrupted reading time, topping up once the tank had reheated. As I said, my sanctuary – and I suppose my escape. When you don't have much money it's the one luxury you can afford. I was willing to talk but knew I couldn't do much else. So when Nelly came in to talk to me one November evening I was ready for another chat. She would tell me who, or what, had been irritating her, what her hopes and dreams were, school problems, job searches, the everyday off-loading of life's little niggles. It was what she had done over the years, sometimes coming in to tell me she was going out, who with, and when she'd be back; or she had already been out and was telling me where she had been and what she had done. She was nineteen, in the house less and less, out working or socialising. She'd always been a bubbly, outgoing and sociable child. If I'd wanted to punish her I'd make her stay in; nothing to her brother who would read, listen to music, watch the TV but the worst punishment ever for Nelly who wanted to be out with friends. She'd been out with friends that day.

She came and stood in the doorway, over my shoulder so I couldn't see her properly. She hovered silently and I knew she wanted to ask me something. She had always been the same when she was unsure of my reaction, lingering on the edges of the room, wondering how to begin – much as I have hovered with my pen over the page, wondering how to begin, where to start.

"Spit it out, Nelly," I said, impatient for her to be gone so I could regain my peaceful oasis. The space between us was a pit of silence. Nothing.

"What do you want?"

Nothing.

Did she need a loan, was she pregnant? Still nothing. I turned to face her.

"What's the matter? Have you bashed the car again?"

She shook her head.

"I need to tell you something…?" her voice trailed as if asking permission to speak. She came closer but didn't sit down.

She was pregnant wasn't she? I could tell by her face, that or in huge debt. Had she run someone over? Oh lord, a car repair was one thing but heaven forbid that she had killed someone. It had to be something major, her face was white, her voice a mere whisper, she kept taking a breath to begin but no words came out. I sat more upright.

"It doesn't matter what it is, Nelly. Tell me and we can sort it out."

She sat on the loo seat, quietly summoning the words.

"I've got a problem. With my eating." She began to cry, quietly, her body trembling, head down, tears dropping onto her lap. I grabbed a towel, stood up, reaching out towards her. It felt like the ground was being sucked away and I would disappear down the plughole. So this was it. I forced myself to stay calm, not to shake. I have no recollection of if I managed it or not, it seems like a dream to me now but I know that I would have fought to remain in control, to be a good mother, to make her know that it would all be alright now, that we would make it better together.

"I'm so scared, Mum, really scared," she managed to say, her body almost collapsed in on itself.

So was I. The room tilted, my world titled with it. I hugged her tightly, never wanting to let her go, wanting to scoop her into my arms as I did when she was small, tell her it would all be OK and have her totally believe me. Even if I didn't believe it myself.

"Don't be scared. Now that I know what it is we can do something about it." How many times had I said those words to my children over the years, totally certain that I could solve all their problems with a bit of clear thinking and a high dose of optimism? Where was that conviction when I needed it most? "Thank you for telling me." I knew how much it had taken for her to confess, the unburdening, the sharing of such news. I held her for a while, her body bony and unresponsive, already that shield, that wall in place. I wanted to weep but I held on, then gradually released her not wanting her to feel trapped or overwhelmed.

"You'll be alright," I said with strength I pulled from somewhere. "Now that we know we can do something about it." I repeated it, to convince myself more than

8

her. At last I knew what enemy I was fighting.

I held her shoulders, kissed her grey face.

"Love you, Mum. I'm sorry, so sorry."

"Nothing to be sorry for."

There wasn't. She hadn't done this on purpose; surely no one would willingly put themselves through such pain and anguish. I just wanted to make it better.

"Let me get dressed and we can talk about it, decide how we can help get you well."

She shook her head. "I'm going out; my friends are waiting in the car."

I forced a smile, encouraged that she still wanted to go out, still had friends that were standing by her. "OK, you go out and I'll see you later."

And off she went. When I heard her car leave the drive I slumped back down into the bath and sobbed. Fear gripped my heart and held it in an iron vice. I was going to lose my daughter. She was going to die, waste away before my eyes. The thoughts were unbearable, running away from me in the darkest of scenarios, a waking nightmare. After a while, all cried out, I set my jaw hard, determination roused. I was not going to let her go. I would not lose my daughter. I would find a way out of this hellish hole and get her well.

My head felt like it was exploding as I rapidly began to make sense of the past few months. The lies, the manipulation she had used to keep her secret hidden. What a fool I felt at that moment. What an idiot. Letting go is the hardest thing, and even after all these years I find it difficult to let go of the fear and shame that gripped me then. And what exactly was her problem with eating? Was it anorexia? Bulimia? Something was so obviously wrong but I didn't then know the extent of it.

I don't remember how long I sat in the bath after that, the flame flickered, blurred by my tears, the water tepid then cold. I roused myself to turn on the hot tap and stayed awhile longer. My daughter was going to die. I was going to die, nothing was as it was, as I thought it would, could, and should be. After months and months of wondering what was wrong with her I finally knew the answer. Why hadn't I known before? Why hadn't I guessed? Because I was stupid, because I was a bad mother, because I was smug, because I had it all together didn't I? No matter what life had thrown at me I had managed to survive, even thrive, and things were finally coming together, we had stability, security, we had our own home, we had everything.

We had nothing. If I couldn't keep my children safe what did we have?

When Nick, our son, had gone off to do his snowboard seasons I had blocked out the fears of him injuring himself, or worse. He would call and tell of avalanches, of friends being airlifted off the mountains. I chose not to think about it, my way of coping. If I didn't think about it, it wouldn't happen, couldn't happen. Simple. I'd heard the phrase 'What you think, you attract', so I didn't think about the risks he was taking – or the consequences – and if he told me I would change the subject. I wonder now whether I was abrupt with him, whether I cut him short to avoid the conversation making deeper my fears – quite possibly, but it was the only way I could cope. Sometimes I tried to convince myself that if anything did happen to him at least he was living his life his way. Some small comfort in the circumstances and thankfully nothing bad ever happened that he couldn't recover from. His snowboarding seasons came to an end when he met Emma and no longer wanted to spend months out of the country. They were busy building their own lives now, settled in a flat, making plans for their future. Neil was flying back and forth to the USA and Mexico. He would spend four or five days at home and then fly back for ten to twelve days. He had noticed the changes in her looks and behaviour and was as worried and concerned as I was. I kept him up to date with progress by telephone and Skype but I felt I needed to free him from any domestic worries so that he could concentrate on business. We always worked as a team, playing to our strengths, I knew I could rely on him and he knew he could rely on me. Minor problems I dealt with and told him afterwards, the major ones we shared and settled on a way forward. We needed a plan. We had to find a way out of this for Nelly – and for ourselves.

Chapter 2: Freefall

Nelly was born in 1989. I had a son, I had a daughter, I was the wealthiest woman in the universe. I had everything. That feeling of euphoria didn't last long. A few months later our life went into freefall at the start of the '90s recession. Our businesses collapsed like a game of computer solitaire, cards tumbling down the screen like butterflies; we handed the keys to our house back to the bank and went to live first with my parents, then in a caravan, followed by a series of flats for a few weeks at a time. Throughout the fear and dread of it all I felt I was lucky because my family was healthy and safe. My nanny always used to say, 'If you've got your health you can work for your wealth.' And wasn't that just so? We had our health, we had each other. We had exactly what we needed. Everything else would come in time. I didn't have much but I had my brain, my wits, my strength and a pig-headed desire not to be beaten. Even though I had suffered bouts of ill health and exhaustion I was a survivor. Now I faltered; would I survive this? Would Nelly survive this?

I had physically felt a metal hand enclose my heart the moment she told me. I thought at the time I was armouring myself, ready to fight. I was not going to lose my daughter. I would not let some insidious disease damage her body. I had been fighting an unknown foe and now that I knew what I was up against I could develop a strategy and beat it. That metal shield took such a long time to divest myself of, even when it was no longer needed. And it wasn't armour, it was a cage, ironclad so that no feeling could come in to hurt me. Not something I would advocate for good mental health but it was the only thing I knew how to do at that time. It was automatic.

For months I had watched her deteriorate, grow thinner, greyer, more lethargic. I had sought help via doctors, specialists, consultants, who found nothing wrong and still she continued to weaken. I went down the alternative route, nutritionists, allergy testing, reflexology – anything and everything. I often wondered afterwards whether they knew and couldn't tell me. Or was Nelly so good at hiding it that they were also none the wiser?

It didn't matter now, her secret had been discovered. She had confessed like an alcoholic who can't be helped until they admit they have a problem. It was out in the open – to me anyway, and I quickly needed to formulate a plan. I had told her we would get through this and I was determined that we would. I had no idea then just how difficult and upsetting that process would be.

So, I sat down on the bed, then flopped onto it, lying in the darkness. Christmas was a few weeks away and three days previous we had been to buy a puppy; a springer spaniel that we had arranged to collect on Christmas Eve. How I regretted that decision now. How would I have the energy and wherewithal to cope with a puppy when every ounce of energy had been drained from me that night? As I cooled down from the bath I grew chilled, goosebumps creeping over my body and I pulled the duvet about me. I didn't want to move, wanted the darkness to swallow me up and keep me safe so that when dawn broke it would all be over. All I could hear was the tick of the clock in another room, the intermittent call of an owl and the sound of my thoughts tumbling uncontrollably in my head.

I needed to tell my husband, I needed to tell our son. What would they say, what would they do? Would they understand? Fear, fear, fear, rising up all the time at what ifs. I wasn't only dealing with my emotions I was pre-empting everyone else's. How would they react? This way or that? And if they did this how would I deflect that? And if they did that how would I counteract it? The whole gamut of reactions was taking charge in my head. I was exhausted already. What should I say? What should I do?

I sobbed again, emptied out, feeling only the cold iron about my heart. I had entered into the madness, down the rabbit hole.

I now had to find the words to tell my husband, Neil, that I finally knew what was wrong with Nelly. And so began the minute calculations of how best to explain things, how best to deal with Nelly, how best for us all – as a family – to find a way out of this latest challenge. In the end I just blurted it out, all the time trying to protect him, warning him to be careful of how we approached this. He was devastated, his little girl, how could he not have known? His instinct was to protect, to make it right, to save her; but we had no idea how on earth we were going to do that, or indeed what to do at all. He cried with me. Later, he held Nelly and cried with her, telling her we would make it right. When she and her brother were small if they hurt themselves he would put his hand over the cut knee, the sore head and say:

Close your eyes.
Now say I wish

I wish
All the pain
All the pain
Would fly in the sky
Would fly in the sky.

And with a sweep of his hand the pain would be gone. How I closed my eyes that day and wished and wished. But the pain didn't fly in the sky.

Chapter 3: The Puppy

And then there was the puppy! Not a calm, passive, handbag dog but a bouncy, energetic springer spaniel. The kids had been working on me for months, trying to persuade me to get another dog and I had caved in. George, our elderly springer, wouldn't last much longer they said and I would be alone in the house. The kids were concerned (ha!) that I needed a companion. Accepting the fact that I would be the one to feed it, clean it, collect the poo and train it, I eventually gave in.

Neil and I had gone to a farm to choose from what was left of the litter, one dog, one bitch. I held them both in my arms, caring nothing that I was in my best coat and they were rolling around, slobbering and sniffing all over it. Choosing one was difficult but in the end, after much deliberating, cooing and soothing, we decided on the bitch, paid the deposit and went off in high expectation of the wonderful surprise it would be on Christmas morning. I was now regretting my decision big time. I really didn't need the additional work and the loss of deposit was nothing in the scheme of things. I knew the stress factor would be sky high anyway, what would a little more add to the load? And it was so cute, and strangely calming. Something told me to go ahead anyway.

This story does have a happy ending (so far), I want to make that clear but it doesn't detract from the fact that the fear switch was flicked onto full steam ahead and from the moment I found out about Nelly's eating disorder I lived in a state of constant anxiety.

We had wanted to get help for Nelly straightaway but she begged me to wait until after Christmas and respectful of her wishes, and with a basic understanding that eating disorders were about control issues, I agreed. I didn't realise that in doing so she was exerting her control over me but in my blind fear I allowed her to do this. She barely spoke to her father about it and most of the conversations about a way forward were between the two of us, as and when she felt able to talk about it. I would then relay what we had discussed to Neil and then he and I would consider our options, what was negotiable and what was non-negotiable. He was always there for me – and for her but he was absolutely devastated. Nelly was her daddy's girl and he felt he had failed her and she felt she had disappointed him. It was a painful experience for all of us but that protective father-daughter bond was fractured and neither of them could find a way to bridge the gap that now appeared between them.

Christmas Eve arrived. I was still sure I could fix what was wrong now that I was aware of it. I had spent the days before reading stuff on the internet, skipping from one website to another, looking for clues, looking for answers. I would find all the information and I would make her well, the perfect solution had to be out there somewhere. For all of my life I have sought answers from books, from the written word. If I wanted to learn something I would get a book about it first, from chess to skiing, someone would have written a book about it. As a child I would seek the answers in the library, so it seemed so natural to do the same now. Someone somewhere would have found themselves in my situation, they would have written about it, dissected and assimilated it and put it in print. How naïve I was. Or was it simply blind hope, a self-protection mechanism kicking in? Girls died of eating disorders, didn't they? Well not my daughter. The answer to all of this was out there somewhere and I was going to find it. The odd thing was that there was nothing in the library and I felt ashamed asking for something in the bookshop. I thought I would be judged and found wanting; that the staff would think 'There goes that dreadful mother who didn't even notice her daughter was ill'.

I trawled the internet hour after hour, looking for advice and scaring myself witless. What I found was both frightening and shocking. There were no filters, no warnings as to what I would discover. There were so many girls, young men, and women, desperate for help to get well. There were also plenty of sites with explicit information given on how to starve yourself, how to cover up your eating disorder, methods of extreme exercise, ways to burn more calories, ways to make yourself sick. So-called Pro Ana sites are legion; how can you keep your child away from them when for the majority of time they can be accessed from the smartphone in the palm of their hand? Also, there were posts from so many people that didn't want to live like this but didn't know how to stop, how to break the pattern. It broke my heart to read about them.

Over the many hours I spent looking for help I researched self-harm and self-abuse. What an eye-opener to discover what is classed as self-harm – nail biting, hair pulling, eyelashes and eyebrows included. Nail biting made me laugh. As a lifelong nail nibbler I thought that was a tad extreme but it made me think how subtle self-abuse is, how accepting we are of it and how the line can be crossed with barely a glance.

That Christmas was the most traumatic I'd ever had. Nothing before or since has come close. All the years of shopping, wrapping and hiding presents was nothing compared to this. Every day was weighted heavy with tension and I dreaded any small hiccup that might make things worse than they already were. I felt time ticking away second by second, wanting to get help but determined to keep my promise to her, afraid that if I left things too long it would be too late.

A couple of days before Christmas a niece posted something on Facebook that sent things spiralling out of control. It was nothing offensive or personal but it triggered a response from Nelly that left her feeling abandoned, ignored, forgotten. It was something so simple, a thank you for a present that hadn't been given, a mere expectation – but these little things can get out of control when 1) you don't have all the facts, and 2) you are living on the edge of a precipice, anticipating possible landmines every minute of every day. Even the smallest of misunderstanding can become explosive and you then get into a habit of over reacting because everything has the potential to become the negative trigger that sends things spiralling out of control. I felt out of control. Whilst I live down south, my parents, my sisters and their families live 300 miles away. I was the only one who had moved from the area. Her distress ignited mine again. I was forgotten too. I felt isolated and abandoned. And yet I had lived apart from them for over twenty years. During that time I had phoned my parents almost every day. Throughout bad times and good my mum and dad had been there for me at the end of the line, many, many times a lifeline that I had clung on to in order to get through. I felt that line slipping through my fingers, burning as it went, leaving a nasty stinging that wouldn't go away. Nelly had arrived home distraught and I called my mum and dad in tears, feeling totally lost and afraid, fearing that I was alone to fight this. I was a small child again, needing the security of someone assuring me that all would be well. I didn't get it. Dad more or less said Nelly was overreacting.

At the time I didn't have all the facts and they didn't know how unstable and fragile the situation was down here. I felt chastised, reverting to my child self, feeling he was choosing my little sister over me, that I was wrong and unreasonable. A *bad daughter* title to add to the list along with failed mother. My other sister came on the phone, soothing me, telling me it would all be OK but I just broke down, the pain was overwhelming.

Fear poured out of me. She was going to die, I knew she was going to die. My sister had experienced her own difficulties and I felt she would understand more than anyone. She too had lived with the daily fear that something dreadful would happen to her child. I managed to calm down but when I eventually hung up I felt more truly alone in the world than I had ever felt. I felt wrong, criticised by the people who loved me most.

They were right of course, I was well and truly caught in the whirlpool Nelly was trapped in, sucking us in deeper and now I felt there was no one to rescue me. I felt so hurt, the pain then was unbearable and I carried that with me for a long time; keeping things on the surface, not wanting to show weakness, not wanting to ask for help, afraid of the criticism which would only reinforce the fact that I was a bad, incapable mother with a bad, incapable child. Nelly needed me. I needed my mum and dad but I didn't like what they said. No one likes the truth.

I don't blame them at all, although I did then, easier to blame someone else, anyone else, someone safe to rail against. I kept phoning them but for a short time it took everything I had to dial the number. The reason I don't blame them is because when you get caught in the madness you become irrational, everything is a threat. I was afraid that I wasn't strong enough to cope with what was to come, and without family support and understanding I feared the worst. Always the worst. Eating disorders are about food, aren't they? Just get her to eat! Exactly what I used to think, never truly understanding the whys and wherefores. How could my parents know? Growing up in the war years, not having what we had now. Couldn't she just pull herself together?

It pains me so much to write this. I love my mum and dad dearly, my sisters too, but just as an eating disorder sufferer pushes all help away so in that moment did I. All the years of being strong, forging forward, collapsed around me. I drew on reserves that I never knew I had – and carried on.

Mum and Dad came to visit soon after Christmas and were there, supporting me as they had done throughout my life, but it took a while to relax again, the pain of being the only bad child, the ungrateful daughter (in my mind) haunted me for a long time, pushing my self-esteem and self-worth even lower than it already was. By the time Christmas had come around and the failures that went with it – the shrunken jumper, the disappointing food; well, there was no wonder my daughter had problems. Who wouldn't if they had a mother like me? The small mishaps took on more significance to me from that point, highlighting all my shortcomings, all the things I got wrong in life. I felt like I was under a huge magnifying glass, sharpening and defining my every move. It began to get exhausting and intimidating and the pressure I put on myself to get my daughter well so that life could return to our 'normal' became intensified.

#

We drove to the farm on Christmas Eve morning to collect the puppy, taking a cardboard box and an old towel for it to nestle against. I had ceased to think with any form of clarity from the moment Nelly told me she was ill so I had made no preparation whatsoever. I had no travel crate, no blanket or bed, simply headed off that morning happy that something wonderful was coming into our life; that small feeling of hope and anticipation keeping me going.

The relief when I saw that scrumptious puppy lifted my hopes higher. She had grown a little but was still only a handful to hold, a liver patch on her head like a bonnet and a couple of little splatters of liver on her body. Her tail had been docked and her dew claws extracted by a vet. This is so important for when exuberant dogs are running through hedges and fences willy-nilly they can catch their claws on brambles and fences. Springers are boisterous and have no sense of decorum, they just plough ahead regardless but if a dew claw gets caught it can rip and tear the leg, causing terrible, painful damage.

She was so utterly gorgeous and I knew in an instant that we would make this work. On the way home we wondered where we could hide her. My garden cabin would be way too cold, the garage store room was also cold but at least we could check on her – except we didn't get the chance. Nick had bought some oysters and insisted he put them in the store room. He saw the puppy immediately. Now the cat was out of the bag – or the dog out of the box. When he came back into the kitchen his wife knew that something was afoot, Nick couldn't hide it from his face. More pressure, Nelly wouldn't want to be the last to know and we couldn't reveal all to everyone else just yet – so we got on the phone to Nelly.

Neil had sent her to get me some last minute flowers, a ruse to keep her out of the way but now we needed her back urgently. She didn't take kindly to being sent on a wild goose chase and then asked to come back as fast as she could through the Christmas traffic. Her face was like thunder when we saw her through the kitchen window and we hoped the 'little excuse' would be enough to diffuse her anger. She came in, slamming her keys down on the kitchen table.

"First you get me going all over Bournemouth looking for roses and now you want me to come back. What's the problem?"

Neil brought the box into the kitchen and set it down on the floor and the little problem poked her head and paws out to see what was going on. Lots of oohs and aahs from everyone else but Nelly burst into tears, fell to her knees beside the box and scooped the bewildered puppy into her arms.

"I was dreading Christmas," she said, all the while

covering the puppy in kisses. "There was no magic left, it was just another day but now it's not. It's special again."

Perhaps this was a sign then that she was having difficulty growing up, taking responsibility, becoming an adult. She had a hard time adjusting to the freedom of choice that comes with leaving the rigidity of school life, enjoyable or otherwise. This in part had restored that magic. One point to us.

"We need to give her a name," I said, inviting suggestions. We wanted something that would pair with George and eventually came up with Millie, which sat well with Nelly and myself and gave the boys a laugh because they immediately thought of the TV programme *George and Mildred*. Mildred became her Sunday name, the name we called her when she peed on the carpet or ate another sock. We remained in the kitchen for most of the evening, besotted with Millie, her cute little face, her adorable eyes, while Nick fussed over George, immediately identifying the usurper as only a first born can.

Christmas is always fraught with tension of some sort but this dissipated it for a while. Although Nelly was struggling we had agreed not to seek help until after Christmas and we kept to our promise, afraid as we were, time ticking rapidly on. Perhaps she wanted to cling onto what remained of our 'normal' and start afresh in the new year. I was certain we could cope and we were as 'normal'. All well and good until I cooked the Christmas Eve ham – except it was undercooked. Fail. The following day I overcooked the turkey. Another fail. The last straw was when I washed a cream Katherine Hamnett cardigan that Nelly had bought from TK Maxx and shrank it. That's when I broke down, unable to stem the flood of tears that I had managed to hold back following that first night when she told me what was wrong. I was an out and out failure, a bad mother, my judgement or rather lack of it was obvious. All the things I had taken as outward signs of my mothering skills had disappeared overnight. It was as if my entire life, everything I valued and thought I'd done well was a lie. A big fat lie.

I felt everything about me unravelled then. I sobbed for the failure I was, for the reality that was not real. For my ideas about myself of being a good mother. Not an excellent or a fantastic mother, but a good enough mother. It was all in my imagination, wasn't it, because how could a good mother not have known? A good mother would have spotted the signs months ago. I was stupid, careless, blind, ignorant. I was useless. Everyone tried to comfort me. "It's only a jumper." But that jumper was my whole life, shrunken and no good to anyone.

In the days that followed I slipped into a dark place. All the things I hadn't done in my life, all the opportunities I hadn't taken because of my duty to my kids, the importance of having a stable family, seemed like a bad joke. It had been for nothing. I could have been more selfish, worked on my career, put my husband and children's needs after mine. What I could have been. Imagined success was mine, all that I imagined I gave up for my family. Great excuse! A great escape! I could procrastinate and hold back my entire life, laying the excuses on my children, if I hadn't had them what could I have been?

The answer is, nothing different. If you're afraid of something whether that be success, change, death, the simple fact is that you're afraid. But it was good to blame. It gave an easy route for my anger and desolation. Now I was well and truly lost. I had failed my daughter, I had failed my son, my husband, but most of all I had failed myself. I wallowed, again in the bath, water level rising with my salty tears. I was in limbo but as soon as Christmas was over we would get this fixed. It was as simple as that.

I barely remember New Year's Eve, dreading what it might bring. As the hour chimed twelve I braced myself, not as I had done other years hoping that all the bad was behind me but this year wondering if I'd be able to survive the next 365 days. Would I still be standing when it came to its end? Would I still have my daughter?

Chapter 4: The Clinic

Nelly told me that her friend had said that if she didn't tell me about her eating disorder he would. He had been home on leave from serving in Afghanistan around the time of her birthday. Thank God for him. No one else had told her that, no one else had given her an ultimatum, a deadline. Only he had had the balls to do it but what was of equal importance was that she knew he would. He called her periodically to chat when he was in Helmand. She had parcelled up a Christmas present to send out to him with jokey underpants and his favourite biscuits among the contents.

I had thought that from the look of her, her grey skin, her hollowed cheeks and bony collar that she was starving herself but as time went on and she managed to tell me a little more I discovered that she wavered between starving herself or bingeing then making herself sick. Her behaviour changed according to her stress levels and how she could manage them at the time. I had been totally unaware of her coping mechanisms. Valuing her privacy cost us dear.

New Year over it was time to get help but where did we go first? I had no idea what help would be available, if any, but guessed the place to start would be our local surgery. I requested a telephone appointment with our doctor. I told him that Nelly had an eating disorder and asked for help and advice. He was immensely kind but explained that as Nelly was over eighteen he would have to speak to Nelly herself (who was cowering in her bedroom as I made the call) before he could take further steps. My immediate thought was that if only she'd told me when it first began I would have been able to take charge but as things stood I had to be a bystander, a coach on the sidelines willing my team to win. I couldn't help but wonder whether things would have been different had she been under eighteen. Would I have been included more? And I wonder whether I would have felt so desperately on the outside of her treatment as I did from that point on. On reflection perhaps that was my lesson to learn as well as Nelly's lesson in life. She could not let go and neither could I. My biggest mistake was that when I handed over the phone for Nelly to speak to the doctor I mentally excluded myself from asking for any medical advice and support I could have benefitted from in order to help her.

I had never thought of myself as a controlling mum, supportive yes, interfering, no. I had made myself available to my kids 24/7 and that was one of my biggest mistakes, I can see that now, but not then. Being available left me open to interruption. I had no boundaries to fall back on, no wall to keep me safe. I was wandering around in an open field, a no man's land, exposed and ready to be shot at.

Whatever help I sought I was constantly met with the same refrain. She was over eighteen, she was an adult. She was, of course she was, but more importantly she was my daughter and I was desperate to get her well. Now I knew, if I didn't before, that I was truly on the periphery. I hated that hollow pain, being shut out; helpless and hopeless. She went to see the doctor who referred her for mental health assessment. That shook me. Mental health? Surely it was just about food. Wasn't it? This was the first inkling I had that an eating disorder was anything but about food.

She got an appointment and we went off to a nearby town, my daughter, her boyfriend and me. It would take forty-five minutes they said. It took an hour and a half. For forty-five minutes I walked around the shops, browsing in charity shops, mindlessly scanning through magazines in newsagents and all the time nervous of what would come next. And what would come next? That was terrifying in itself and I desperately fought not to let my thoughts run away creating different outcomes. It was important to stay focussed on the here and now and I returned to the waiting room and spent the following forty-five minutes reading the posters, the pamphlets and the health and safety notices in the waiting room, trying to quell the churning in my stomach. In my pocket I had stashed a large bag of Maltesers that I munched through, hoping for chocolate sedation.

Eventually, I was called in to a cramped office; Nelly sat one side of a small desk and two women sat at the other. They asked me to sit down. Nelly didn't look at me, didn't say a word all the time I was in there. They explained that they would refer Nelly to Kimmeridge Court. I made a mental note to Google it as soon as I got back. They also explained that Nelly would receive treatment there. And that was it. Nothing else, no information, no list of things to do or not to do, no guidance, no support, no answers. I had thought that something would happen that day, that they would send me to the equivalent of A & E. That there would be a quick and effective cure, a plaster on the arm, a return in six weeks, end of. I have no idea of what was said to her in that room and I am sure that Nelly will remember nothing such was her state of mind at that time. I know that I behaved bright and optimistic, upbeat and reassuring while Nelly, grey and silent, slid into the car beside her silent boyfriend. The burden of everything I was carrying just got heavier.

We went home with nothing to tell and nothing to do but wait, my positivity and hope depleting with each movement of the minute hand on the kitchen clock.

The appointment arrived quicker than I expected but still what had seemed like an age, and Nelly braced herself for whatever was to happen next. We all did.

The day of the appointment was as tight as a scar with tension; we were all desperate for something to happen, something or someone to guide us through these unchartered waters. We all bundled into the car, Neil and myself up front, Nelly between her brother and her boyfriend squashed in their winter layers, and drove to the clinic, radio loud to break the heavy silence of anticipation. Nick was adamant that if they didn't do anything he would barricade himself into an office and refuse to move until someone did something. His desperation was palpable, possibly witnessing the effect on me and Neil, desperate to retain a sense of normality – to make me better?

My brain raced with possibilities as we drove along. Would they take her in? That would be a relief as we could hand the problem over to the experts. And if they did, how long for? Where would she stay? When would we visit? What would we do? What were their methods? Laughable really, because to this day I have no idea what the treatment is or was. Part of me wanted them to admit her because I was exhausted with worry and stress and another part of me feared that if they took her in we might never see her again. Perhaps they wouldn't help at all, perhaps she wasn't ill enough yet. This was far and above the worst option, because then there would be more fighting, more research, more, more, more and I had nothing left. I needed to sleep a long dark sleep and awaken when it was all over and Nelly was well again.

I have to admit here that a part of me feared the stigma of mental health hospitals and can confess my ignorance wholeheartedly. It's something we need to conquer because if we don't, people will continue to avoid seeking good help.

As we drew into the car park Nelly started to cry, her jaw jutted as it had done when she was a child and unwilling to cooperate. This was not going to be easy, it never was, but now she was harder to handle, harder to coax out of the car and into the building. I couldn't pick her up and carry her but I'd give it a damn good try.

We opened the doors to get out and she refused to move. I instantly felt that familiar adrenaline surge as I fought not to panic. We tried gentle coaxing and when that didn't work I told her that if she didn't get out and walk I would drag her out. She got out. Immediate guilt on my part that I shouldn't have shouted, should have kept my cool but we had an appointment and time was against us. I was not going to let her miss it. I had respected her wishes over Christmas and now she had to pay her part of the deal. We were going into that clinic no matter what.

In the end we had to prise her out of the car, almost drag her to the door. I rang the bell and we waited to be let in. The receptionist spoke to us through an intercom and then released the door. We stumbled into a small waiting room with three plastic chairs, a small Formica table and a water cooler. I felt that my heart was pounding so fast that it would burst altogether from the pressure. Simply walking into that waiting room was such a monumental relief and, most helpful of all, there were plenty of posters and pamphlets for me to read. The answer had to be on there somewhere.

Someone came and took Nelly through to another room and the four of us waited. Chatting, silent, reading old copies of *Caravan* magazine and *Newsweek* that were piled haphazardly on the table, sipping water, stepping out for air, thumbing messages on phones. No one came to talk to us to let us know what was going on or to offer advice. When her session was over she was brought through to the waiting room by one of the staff who said she would see her next week. She didn't reply, walked solemnly to the door and we followed her and drove home.

Was I relieved or was I disappointed? Both I suppose, relieved that she was coming home and petrified of the responsibility of caring for her. I was struggling to get her to eat, watchful that she didn't then vomit it up. It wasn't so much that she was so very thin that there was danger of her organs collapsing more that now the secret was out in the open that her options became more severe. I would lie awake each night, hoping she was safe, that she was asleep. Many nights I heard her pacing about in her room. It strikes me now that it's the familiar feeling of being a new mum and not knowing how to begin to care for a baby that is totally reliant on you for its survival. The enormity of responsibility is terrifying. At least then there are other people to ask for advice and you muddle through, gaining confidence once you have survived that first few nights when you stay awake listening for every breath. The baby stays in one place. Not so with an adult teenager who can drive, that has a job, that you have no control over whatsoever. And there is no one to ask what to do, what not to do. You are on your own. Not only that but other people are looking to you for guidance. Neil and Nick were constantly asking what was going on, what they should do, what was I doing, how they could help, how they should react? I had as little knowledge as they did. It was a huge learning curve for all of us. If they'd taken her in as a patient would that have been any better? All I know is that perhaps it would have given me a break from the constant anxiety of wondering where she was, and if she was safe.

Looking back I'm glad she came home but fear and panic had well and truly taken its hold on me. Adrenaline rushed around my body without a break. I was hyper alert – was she OK? Was she eating? What could I do to make her well? I still have no idea what was said at that meeting, nor all subsequent ones. That is, and was, between Nelly and her therapist but at the time it was bleak and frightening. As I was to realise later, you can't take care of your child forever, you have to let them grow and learn and wobble and fall. You have to stand back while they hurt because you cannot take the hurt for them however much you'd like to. I was on a path just as Nelly was. Perhaps we would meet somewhere in the middle. I have the objectivity of the past now, of lessons learned. I can see my fear, feel the fear of how it was, only now am I beginning to process my part in it all. I hope by doing so I can help others stand and bear the pain of separation. Brutal as it was, it was time to stand back and let others help her and to let her help herself. I could only do what she allowed me to do, and guess, guess, guess at what was the *best* thing to do.

Nelly's memories of that time are vague; she was expert at blocking things out. I wonder where she learnt that from as a coping strategy? Again, guilty as charged.

Self-worth is a funny thing. It's not other people who make us feel bad about ourselves, most of us are quite capable of doing so without help from anyone else. No one told me, ever, that I was a bad mother. I told myself that I was.

My mum used to joke that when she had me she lost some of the curl from her hair, that she stopped having so much milk in her tea – and that she didn't swear until she had me. I filtered this as turning my beautiful mother into a straight haired, black tea drinking, foul mouthed freak. She's not (she wasn't the last time I looked anyway). My sister was the funny, adventurous one and by the time she got to the youngest of us three girls, well, she was nigh on perfect. This was my filter. All the bad things happened when I was born. As far as I know they can't put you in prison for making your mother swear and I'm pretty sure my dad gave her cause to swear a lot more than I ever did. I asked her – he did!

My parents also told me how clever I was, how creative, how I had natural rhythm, I could be a dancer, how bright, how I could do anything I wanted to, be anything I wanted to be. I passed the eleven-plus, wasn't I brilliant? I could draw, I could do lots of things but like many people I didn't focus on those things, they were muffled in the background, because really, I was a bad girl. I cried a lot. All that stuff and nonsense lay bubbling underneath and when something went wrong it all bubbled up again, ready to reinforce the fact that I was indeed a bad person, a bad mother. My parents were always encouraging, supportive, loving, always made we three girls believe we could do anything we wanted to do if we worked hard. I did work hard but if you feel deep down that you are a bad person you will never feel worthy of good things.

Most of all I felt that I had been found out. That all the time I thought was a good mother, a caring, vigilant mother, I was pretending, and I had got caught out.

So I was desperate to get out of this mess, find a way to save my daughter, and prove that I was a good mum after all. When I look back at all the things that happened then and during the next few years there was no wonder I fell into a depression, not that I was aware of it, but when I started to note all the things that went on there was no wonder I hit a brick wall and couldn't get over or around it.

# # #

And so Nelly began her outpatient treatment, going to clinic once a week. I would drive her there and we would walk slowly to the entrance where I would ring the buzzer for access because she couldn't bring herself to do it. How could you not ring a buzzer and speak up? I now know that I should have made her ring it, waited for as long as it took but at that time I was afraid to make her do it for herself. Gentle coercion made her panic, and fearful that she wouldn't go in at all I would ring and ask for access through the speaker phone. Then we would sit and wait until she was called into the room and I would sit and wait until she was finished. I'd learned to take my own magazines to keep me occupied as the only thing I ever found on the table was *Caravan* and *Motor Home* and dated copies of *The Week*. Nelly suggested that maybe this was because they didn't have any pictures of 'perfection', of perfect celebrities, of people with perfect lives. I began seeing magazines in a new light after that. Even my monthly subscription of *Good Housekeeping* and *Woman & Home* contained fashion pages of perfection, homes of perfection, children of perfection, careers of perfection. Perfection, or the illusion of it, was everywhere. Sometimes I took a magazine, always I took water and a thermo-mug of coffee. Mostly I was there for an hour or more, sometimes two, sitting, waiting, wondering what was happening behind closed doors. Wondering what Nelly was saying, wondering how they were helping her, wondering how we would find our way out of the maze.

Over the weeks and months that I sat in the waiting room I saw many other people come and go. Most were thin, painfully thin, grey girls, a few women, one young man. Some were larger than average (what is average?) but not so obviously thin or ill. I saw mothers like myself with their daughters and recognised that same haunted look, blank and unseeing on the sufferer, blank and disbelieving in the parent. No one spoke, only smiled or averted their gaze altogether. It was heartbreaking watching these beautiful girls sit in silence, staring at the floor, waiting their turn and I wondered what drove them to this vile situation. I once saw a mother and daughter and it was hard to tell who the patient was as they were both so very thin. The mother was perfectly groomed, the father sat waiting in a deluxe car in the car park. Women in their thirties and forties arrived in open-topped cars, dressed head to toe in designer clothes, expensive handbags and jewellery, outwardly bearing the badges of success, and inwardly? Who knows, I certainly don't, I can only guess as I continue to question what makes someone go down this slippery path. It was all assumption on my part but I could only sit and ponder what made these women so unhappy that they could inflict such pain and sadness on themselves and, as a consequence, on those who loved them.

Chapter 5: Distraction

Once I'd read all the posters and pamphlets and bored myself with the magazines I began to take some writing with me. I didn't want Nelly to think she was wasting my time sitting there, something else for her to feel guilty about, something else for her to punish herself for. I wanted to demonstrate that I was strong, determined, that I was doing something for myself, looking forward to the future. I would write the novel I was always talking about. So each week I would take an A4 notebook, a fistful of coloured felt pens and work at it, chapter by chapter. Head down, scribbling away, more than once I was mistaken for some kind of professional which made me smile. I was the biggest amateur blundering around in the dark, trying to make sense of this nightmare. So many times I sat in the waiting room, wondering what was being said. Not that I was bothered that it was anything about me, or anything I had to hide. I didn't fear the revealing of secrets or anything else for that matter I just wanted to know what to do. I still thought there was one perfect answer, a secret code, that if I knew what was troubling her I could fix it. An extension of the mum who helps their child to read and write, support them with their homework, soothes their nightmares, nurses them through measles and chickenpox, protects them from bullies and puts plasters on their scuffed knees. If only this had been so simple. Week after week I sat there, jacket on against the winter cold and then T-shirt or short sleeves as summer came. Eventually she would drive herself there but for many months I sat in the waiting room, trying to be composed and serene, and feeling anything but.

And through all of this I wrote my first novel, a distraction, something to aim for, something that would have an end, a happy ending. It was what I needed. There are many pages of notes, many drafts on the laptop, edits, changes, but editing and changing my life was not so easy to shape. I sought to control my imaginary world because I was afraid of what was happening in the real one. It seems odd to me that I couldn't write about what was going on in my life when I had always done so before. Every morning for years I had written three pages of A4, writing about what had happened, what I hoped would happen, planning my day, emptying my head of all life's niggles so that I could write creatively. It was therapy and yet when I needed it most I couldn't do it, couldn't get started. Perhaps it was so hard living the jumble that it hurt too much to face up to it on the page, the abject failure of my life, as a parent, too painful. So I avoided it altogether, preferring my imaginary world. I must have written something but nothing remains except one page in a book that I started, hoping to keep note of her progress, which was swiftly abandoned. Writing about it made it more real and I honestly couldn't face up to the fact that my life was once again taking a downward turn.

Distraction can be a lifesaver. Many of the parents I spoke to afterwards, when I was braver and more able to seek support, found their own distractions – going out with friends, knitting, taking a new class, a new course; something that was absorbing and needed their full attention. In doing so they found a small respite from the grind of either looking after or worrying about their child. It's so easy to shut yourself away, isolate yourself from friends and family but in most circumstances that's the worst thing you can do. You need to be a part of the world not shut off from it. You need to guard against it from the very beginning.

Chapter 6: The Other Side

Most sessions, while we waited for Nelly's appointment, people came and went and Nelly gave me an insight as to the subtle sights and signals around me. "Hey, Mum, check out the girl who jiggled her legs continuously while waiting to be seen," not as I thought with anxiety, but in an attempt to burn off calories. That the girl, so thin she was in a wheelchair, was there not because she couldn't walk but because she would burn less calories that way. All quite innocuous things to me but here I was having my eyes opened again. Was I so blind? Naïve? I began to doubt everything I saw, looking for the underlying message it was surely presenting to me.

Sometimes during my penitence, as time passed and the weather became warmer, I stepped outside for air. The waiting room was glass on two sides and quickly became hot and stuffy. Seagulls would wander around outside looking for scraps – perhaps aware that they wanted the food more than the people inside.

After mind numbing, tedious waiting Nelly would burst into the waiting room once again. She would get in the car, stern faced, silent. After a while I would venture, "Everything alright?" and she would launch into a tirade about how stupid it all was, what a bitch her therapist was. On and on she would rant, letting off steam until eventually she would quieten. I daren't pry, daren't rush or ask too many questions in case I did or said the wrong thing, undoing all the work that the session had done beforehand. Nelly would let rip about one thing or another and when I thought the time was right I would calmly suggest:

"Do you think she might have a point though?" and off she would go again. This went on for numerous weeks, me sweating and tense as I drove, contained within the metal capsule of the car, anticipating the subsequent explosion, and with no escape. That was until one week, as we negotiated a large roundabout I decided to go all the way around, once, twice, three times and when Nelly realised what I was doing she began to laugh, we both did, releasing all the tension. There were quite a few roundabouts on the way home and occasionally, when the emotional temperature was getting too high I would drive three times around the roundabout. I did it once when my husband was with us and he thought I'd lost the plot, moaning about the waste of petrol, which made us laugh even more. And it was in those moments that I realised I was finding a way to help Nelly navigate through this mental storm, that I had come up with ways to break the tension and diffuse the enormity of what we were going through. Laughter was definitely part of my armoury and we were to use it often.

Chapter 7: Millie

Of course, you must be wondering about the puppy. Millie was, as I suppose all puppies are, the cutest thing ever. Despite the added stress of luminous yellow puddles on my cream carpet, chewed furniture and socks – among other things – she was a joy to have around. We survived Christmas Eve night, ignoring the howling and whining while we slept – or tried to. She soon settled in and became part of the family, much to the irritation of our old dog George, another springer. I know; we are gluttons for punishment. For a dog on his 'last legs' he soon perked up at the competition for 'Best Dog'. Millie baited and jumped on him and he didn't move a muscle, chillin' and relaxin', but when it came to a belly rub or a biscuit he would trample over his opponent without a second glance. Millie would fall asleep resting her head on his back or nestled close beside him. They were good for each other and as a consequence good for us. They set a great example, rubbing along despite their differences, curled close in front of the fire, together.

We, or perhaps I, yes, it was definitely I, managed to get her toilet trained remarkably quickly and as soon as she had had her injections we signed up for Puppy Training and Socialisation Classes, known as Puppy Parties. The first six weeks were the socialisation classes, getting her used to other dogs. As an exercise this turned out to be an abject failure but one I learnt to laugh about. Not all failures are bad. She was perfectly fine in the car, sitting on the back seat with Nelly for the duration of the fifteen-minute drive, happily looking out of the window but as soon as we reached the vet's surgery she morphed into something else entirely. None of the dominance and bravado she showed at home with George, oh no, she became the most timid and fearful puppy that ever lived, spending the entire session under the chair and wouldn't come out under any circumstances. No treat, no encouragement was enough to coax her to join in. The other puppies ran around, sniffed and played with each other but not Millie. Millie was on retreat, she wasn't coming out for anyone. We would get her doing the tasks only if the other dogs were on leads and close to their owners. It struck me that her behaviour mirrored Nelly's, that although she was prepared to join in with things she preferred to do it in small stages, in her own time – and bribery was impotent.

Each week we would learn some new aspect of puppy care, of what and what not to feed them, how to clean their ears and teeth, simple basic care procedures. There was a show off cocker spaniel that did everything that was asked of it and more, perfectly. We didn't like that dog, nor consequently its smug owner. We were locked in a war against perfection in all its guises, animal or human. That Millie hid under the chair made us love her more. She was hiding away from the overwhelming busyness of the world and so were we.

Those short drives to puppy training, the tension of the waiting room at the clinic, gave Nelly and me something to bond over. It was an appointment, a fixture that we had to look forward to and focus on – and it was fun. We had a guaranteed laugh each week and we really needed to laugh. It was also something we did together, just the two of us, keeping a connection. It was always a choice, she didn't have to come but she did and that was such a boost. Was it more for me than for her? I don't know but at least while she was with me I knew she was safe and I didn't have to worry. I see now that it was the perfect escape, an allotted, structured time each week that she had to commit to and looked forward to. It was not something she had to do but something she chose to do, with me. It was something to focus on.

And so every week we would set off, discussing what funny things we expected to happen each time. Millie soon learnt to sit quietly on the back seat, looking out of the window and she didn't move around or whine the whole way as George would have done and we felt a measure of pride at our success. We had the chance to put things right with Millie. A fresh start.

After that we progressed to puppy training part two, which was when the fun really began. The sessions took place in a village hall a good thirty-minute drive away, down winding, tree-lined country roads in the pitch black of winter evenings. I don't remember the majority of what we even talked about on those journeys but I do know that we talked and didn't sit there in awkward silence. We would talk about what we expected to do that evening, and whether our darling Millie would be best dog.

I would urge everyone to attend a puppy training class. Even if you don't have a dog, borrow one just for the experience. We had such a laugh. There was a farting greyhound that we tried to avoid sitting next to at all costs. A totally disinterested dog that would get up, walk to a spot then lay down and refuse to move an inch. We were encouraged to take small treats to give to

the dog as a reward, dog treats, cheese, biscuits, bits of
sausage or chicken. A family came each week with a
large bag of cheese that they proceeded to eat
themselves. And there were always puddles; the mop
came out more than once each session and that was
another bonus in a weird way. Puppies are learning
everything, they get nervous, they may have an
accident; it is no big deal. We went from worrying if
our dog would be the naughty dog and pee – or worse
– to not even noticing whether a dog did or didn't
shame themselves. We try and we fail, and that's what
life's all about. Somehow we have to keep going until
we get the task completed.

Each week the trainer would demonstrate a task
with her own dog, then we would all move onto the
floor, find a space and work with our own dog. Getting
them to sit, stay, come, leave it, walk to heel, walk on a
lead and off. It was a work in progress – as were we. It
gave us time together doing something different and
new, working together, our focus on Millie, not on
food, not on the drama being played out the rest of the
time.

Kate, Nelly's therapist, told her that I had been very
clever getting a dog, getting Nelly to care for it, for
someone to rely on her for food and safety. There was
nothing clever about it other than perfect timing but if I
ever find myself in a similar situation I would
definitely get a dog. Dogs very quickly become part of
the family; they are loyal and true, happy to see you
morning, noon and night, wanting to be as close as
possible, wanting to be loved. During difficult times in
life they are a huge comfort. You can tell an animal all
your troubles knowing that they will never breathe a

word to anyone, never betray you. They are such good listeners, they never interrupt, nuzzling closer when you need it owing to some marvellous sixth sense they possess. Millie was also very good for me. She was the distraction and comfort I needed.

Everything was a positive then as regards to getting a puppy until the day she went missing. George was old but still adventurous, there was plenty of life and mischief left in him; he would find every gap in the fence and attempt a break-out to determine what was occurring in the big wide world. Once he'd discovered it was nothing much except a series of wee markings here and there he would come back after a few minutes. Foxes and badgers often burrowed holes between the neighbour's fence and ours so we regularly had to inspect for gaps and block them up with soil, planks, bricks and anything else that we could find in the garden. We were always vigilant that when we let Millie out we stayed with her at all times – all of us except Neil who would go outside leaving the door slightly ajar, enough to enable George to push at it with his nose and let himself out, Millie following close behind. One Saturday morning he did this and George disappeared, swiftly followed by Millie who seized the opportunity to find out what lay beyond the fence. George returned in due course but Millie was nowhere to be seen. In a matter of minutes we had lost her. Our garden is bordered by heathland, full of gorse, heather, pine trees and fox and badger sets. We were soon all in the garden, calling out, shouting down the holes. Neil and Nelly ran down the road at the front of the house and I ran onto the common, acres of it, shouting her name. Not even a whimper in response. After an hour we were desperate and tearful. What if a fox got her, or a badger? We trawled the common for a couple of hours but to no avail, no one we spoke to had seen her. They promised to look out for her and we told them all where we lived. I felt deranged as I raced up and down the slopes, losing my footing in the sandy soil. I must have looked odd, shouting down holes and into the air but I didn't care. We couldn't lose her, we just couldn't.

Desperate for help we searched for a photo of her, got on the computer and made a poster, and the whole time I was trying to stem the panic rising inside of me. What if we didn't find her? What if we did and it was too late? I was cursing the computer, the leaflets weren't printing fast enough; we were losing time. I forced images from my mind, scenarios of what could happen. I was getting good at this after all, I could block out almost anything now. Nelly had formed such a bond with Millie, it was helping her so much. If anything happened to Millie what would happen to Nelly? Would it all spiral out of control just when I thought we were getting somewhere? Perhaps I wasn't so much upset about losing Millie as to what would happen to Nelly if we did.

Posters printed we set off on our doorstep campaign, fixing them to our gateposts and strategic points along the way – the entrance to the common where the dog walkers came and went, lamp posts, fences. We knocked on doors and if no one answered put a poster through the letter box. We got to know a lot of our neighbours that day, a couple of disinterested ones but mostly helpful, kind people who we'd never spoken to before. They went out of their way to help, phoning if they heard a yapping, inviting us to search their gardens. One little boy set off like Sherlock Holmes hunting the street for clues but despite all our best efforts at the end of the day we had nothing to report, not one sighting. It was sobering to make that first contact with so many people that lived down our road. People we wouldn't know if we passed them on the high street, yet all were willing to help. And so kind.

At around 6.30pm a neighbour from one of the houses backing onto our road called to say they'd heard a whining. We dashed round in the car, scoped the garden, calling out, listening; but no sound came back. As night fell a neighbour next door but two said she'd heard a dog yapping. We went out searching her large garden in the darkness stumbling as we went, a shared torch between us. There was not one sound we could attach to that of a puppy and all the while the neighbour made her concerns known, loudly.

"Well, if the foxes get him they'll rip him to shreds just for sport, that's what they do," and, "It's so cold, it's freezing, you'd wonder whether a young dog could survive."

Everything she said made me panic even more. Was she filling Nelly's head with pictures of Millie being savaged by foxes? And yet my thoughts were exactly the same as hers. I just didn't want to say them out loud for speaking them would make them more real, more likely to happen.

In the end, our search fruitless, we thanked her and went home and Nelly left to spend the night at her boyfriend's house.

I drifted in and out of patchy sleep, the windows wide open, hearing the rustle of leaves, counting the times foxes, deer and badgers tripped the security lights as they moved around the garden. I rose early, determined to find her with the same single-mindedness I had that Nelly was going to get well. I would not be defeated, I would not fail, I would find Millie, and I would find her healthy and well. The sun was already up; it was bright, fresh and still very cold. Sunday morning was quiet, no hum of distant traffic from the main roads, too early for most people to be up and about and that helped me tune in to different sounds.

I went out, still in my pyjamas, and called Millie's name a few times, concentrating on the direction in which calls had indicated she was earlier. I listened with strained ears for any noise that might alert me that she had found her way home. After two or three calls I heard a bark, and it was most definitely from a young dog. Desperate to locate the direction it had come from I called again. No sound. Still, it had definitely been Millie's bark, I was certain of it. I ran back inside, dressed, pulled on some shoes, ran to the front of the house, called again, desperate to hear her bark but conscious that it was Sunday morning and most people would be having a lie in. Nothing was going to hold me back now; I would find that dog no matter what. Nelly's well-being, if not her life, depended on it. It might seem over dramatic now but that was how I felt, walking a tightrope, trying to remain strong, positive and upbeat, once again blocking out what might happen. I would find that dog and bring her home and we would have that happy ending.

Nelly called from her mobile, she was walking through the woods to our house in case she found Millie there. I told her about the bark and she rushed up to meet me.

We walked in the direction of the bark, listening, calling gently. After about three houses down I was beginning to think I was mistaken. Then I heard Millie whine. As we got to the fifth house I looked over the garden wall and there she was, trembling, sat in the middle of the drive. I was elated but she wouldn't come to me. Nelly and I crouched down, trying to coax her but she wouldn't move. I stood a little, held my breath, moved forward and she shot into the hedge that ran alongside the owner's garage. I felt sick. We could lose her again, she could wiggle in the gaps to the gardens beyond and we wouldn't be able to follow her, into the next garden, nearer to the main road at each turn. It would take time to go back for the car, even longer to run around, such was the design of the cul-de-sacs. I reached forward, she sat quivering within the hedge. As I grabbed for her she yelped and squealed and I was certain the owners would be up at their bedroom window, wondering what the hell I was doing in their garden. I swept her up into my arms and we ran home. Nelly stayed with her in the kitchen while I ran upstairs to Neil.

"I've got her, she's back," I cried. He leapt out of bed, ran downstairs without his glasses and wondered why he couldn't see. We were joyous and laughing, no one was to blame, she was safe and all was well with the world.

Chapter 8: Missing the Signs

Although I was now becoming aware of everything Nelly said to the nth degree, it made me wonder how I had missed the signs before she revealed her eating disorder to me, if indeed there were such signs to spot. Of course there were the obvious indications of her being ill; she looked grey and gaunt, she professed stomach aches, sickness, not being able to eat. I took her to the doctors who referred her to specialists, we saw consultants who could find nothing wrong, which was in a way reassuring and baffling at the same time. No one had an answer for me. I dreaded she had leukaemia or something dire as she was so ill and listless, there had to be something they were missing. I paid for a nutritional therapist to come to the house who advised a healthy diet and eating from small bowls so portion sizes would not be overwhelming, to eat small and often. I drove her to Weymouth to have allergy testing on recommendation from a friend and got myself tested at the same time. Nelly was always afraid and nervous before these events and I see now that she was afraid someone would discover the truth about her eating disorder before she had a chance to tell me herself – but if they did make that discovery they never let on. I didn't think her nerves unusual. She had always been nervous and timid when starting something new. She loved school but after a week off for half-term she would panic about going back as if it was her first ever day there. This appeared to be no different and with a measure of kindness, coercion and firmness I would manage to get her to do things.

All the time I was wondering what could be wrong

with her – I knew something wasn't right – and how I was going to fix it. I was always so sure I could fix anything that it never once occurred to me that I wouldn't have the capability or the answer; that Nelly had to fix herself. A friend visited with her husband who was a reflexologist and he gave her a treatment but didn't raise any concerns.

Wherever I turned I could find no answer. I didn't think for one second that she would have an eating disorder, the thought never crossed my mind. She had always had a fantastic appetite, there had never been a problem in getting her to eat. No finicky fussy eaters in my house. Apart from 'he likes peas, she doesn't, she likes cucumber, he doesn't', the kids ate heartily and well, and they both knew how to cook. I had always involved them when preparing simple meals or baking cakes. We lived a short walk from the school, no more than ten minutes, but if I ever walked to collect her at 3.00pm and didn't take a snack with me she would cry all the way home and say she was starving. Four and half years younger than her brother she could match him plate for plate, never overweight, always active, always doing something, out playing with friends at every opportunity; she loved sport, fearlessly climbed high into the trees about the house while I nervously tried to coax her down. I clearly remember saying to her that I was never worried that she'd get an eating disorder because she loved her food too much. How stupid can you be? But that was when I thought eating disorders were about food. For the moment I could only concentrate on searching for clues.

I had never been one to fuss about my weight, didn't go on weird and wonderful diets, didn't moan that I was too fat or too thin. I kept active by walking the dog and gardening and if my clothes became too tight I cut back a little, paid more attention to what I ate. Other than that I wasn't obsessive about anything to do with food or weight.

I tried hard to work out when it all began, when I'd noticed the trouble with food. We moved to our present house in 2007 and before that in our previous house I can remember her making a pan of pasta and tomato sauce. Competent enough to cook from scratch she didn't have to rely on cans and jars. In the last few weeks of living in that house she got a new boyfriend who was coeliac. She would be concerned about his food when eating with us, panicking a little, watching over me to make sure I didn't use flour, contaminate things with crumbs of bread. She became hyper aware, afraid for some reason, thinking he would die or get cancer and it would be her fault. On one occasion my parents were visiting and we were having a barbeque; she was edgy that the grill would be contaminated but I dismissed her behaviour as over-reactive teenage stuff. Maybe I should have paid more attention; but if I had, what else could I have done?

Even so, I became an avid label reader finding out what products contained gluten and bought gluten free when I could to keep the stress minimal. I considered myself a good host. I was being kind and considerate, that's all.

Was this the start of it escalating when before it had been a slight undercurrent? Hard to tell; with all addictions and mental health problems, it never starts with just one thing but an accumulation of many, a perfect storm. There had been an incident with a boy when she was around fifteen; she had been badly bullied and ostracised at school, much of the bullying taking place in the canteen, an area where food was the focus. Were these the triggers?

Her move to the upper school seemed to be the beginning of the slippery slope. After loving both first and middle school experiences, joining in with everything, happy and thriving, she became a child who stepped away from things. She loved music but was taught alongside a total beginner so that she became bored and dropped it altogether. Had she kept at it would it have been her saving grace? I used to think so but I don't any more.

I don't think there are safety nets that can help a child avoid this. So many talented kids manage to pass exams with perfect grades, play sport at high level, be creative, and still lose their way. There are so many what ifs and maybes but the result was, that due to a combination of things or perhaps only two, Nelly sought to control her world through eating – or rather through not eating.

She was clever at hiding things, something that became clear from other parents I spoke to, books I read, articles I found in print and on the internet. She hid her body with oversized clothes, baggy jeans and jumpers. Boyfriend jeans, sloppy joes and hoodies were in fashion so I didn't see her shape changing at all. I loved wearing sloppy joes myself at her age because, as with most fashion trends, they were doing the rounds when I was a teenager; there is, after all, nothing new, just a different revolution of the circle, variations on a theme. I had loved the comfort, the lack of restriction. I had never once considered it was part of a deception.

She took to walking to her boyfriend's house two miles away. I didn't think anything odd about that either. I walked a lot when I was younger, craving the solitude, the time and space to think. Sometimes I thought it was because she didn't want me to have to drive her there, put me out. Or could it be that she didn't have cash for petrol for her own car or was saving money. Not once did I think it was about burning calories. I feel so stupid now, missing the cumulative signs, but it was all so subtle, all so plausible. And I was distracted, after years of renting I was finally back in a house I owned and I was throwing myself into making it a home. And Nelly was manipulative, as those with eating disorders are; she needed to keep her secret safe and would do whatever it took for it not to be discovered. There is so much of the smoke and mirrors they deploy that deflect you this way and that to distract your attention, and it's easy for our adult children to hide things they don't want us to know. As a parent you want them to grow, to take charge of their lives and so you find yourself in a dilemma from the start. How much do you, and can you, interfere?

After years of struggling, losing our house in the '90s recession, we had finally been able to buy our own home after years of renting, moving six times in five years. Her dad was away a lot of the time, flying back and forth, her brother had gone off to do a ski season, met a girl, got serious and settled down, moved out. Our new home was safety and security at last. We had been there for two years and for two years Nelly had been ill, slowly going downhill and I had no idea why. Most of the time it was just me and Nelly, more often just me and the dog because she was always out. She'd met a boy and it seemed serious. After all the years of turmoil I thought that our struggles were over, that we had hit a smooth patch for a change and could cruise along for a while but now we had another fight on our hands and this was one I wasn't sure I could win. Nothing had prepared me for this. Losing your home is one thing, losing a child is quite another. My worst fear.

Chapter 9: Losing it

When Nelly was born my life was as I had always wanted it to be. Dreams fulfilled. I had planned to complete my family before I was thirty (I was two months shy of twenty-nine); I had a beautiful home, a wonderful husband and a gorgeous, gentle son. I would soon have it all. Everything. When she was placed in my arms I thought the world was perfect, and my life was too. How lucky was I to have so much?

Within a year we had lost our house, our cars, our businesses and were living with my parents. It was a dreadful time for us and it took us twenty years to finally be able to buy our own home again. I will never forget the feeling of knowing we wouldn't have to rent any more, didn't have to move again. A castle, a fortress was ours at last. Now we could unpack everything. The time we got back into our home was the time Nelly's illness tightened its grip.

When she told me she had an eating disorder my immediate thought was that I would lose her, that the circle of our life was complete. I had given birth to her and lost our home and stability, now that we had it back again would we lose our daughter? I realised then how fragile that new-found security was. I had longed for our own house, convinced that I would feel safe and secure once I had it. Now I know that safety and security is something we have within ourselves and never will find it elsewhere no matter how hard we search for it. I learned such a lot through this illness that I never dreamed of.

I'm still not aware of many things Nelly did to hide her eating disorder but this is some of the stuff I did discover. The sad fact is that I dismissed them all as perfectly normal teenage behaviour. I found a diet book, a calorie counter, thought nothing of it. I calorie counted as a teenager, I didn't develop an eating disorder. She had left some diuretic tablets in her car door that I happened to see when I borrowed her car. I didn't think anything of that either; I had used them myself with premenstrual bloating. All these things were part of growing into womanhood, of being uncomfortable in your own body, getting accustomed to having breasts, a waist and hips. It never occurred to me that Nelly would never have an eating disorder that I couldn't put all these things together and discover what is now so glaringly obvious. Was it double denial? I'm not sure even now that I missed the signs, it was all so plausible. She would say she was eating at her boyfriend's house, her friend's house, had had a takeaway. Neil was flying in and out of the country, I was making a home, writing, living quietly at last and had no idea that things had got so bad. Was I deluded in my happiness? I don't think so. After speaking to many parents most of them will say the same which was a comfort of sorts, I didn't feel so stupid after that, stupid yes – but not *so* stupid! I didn't understand the enormity of what she was doing but thankfully I did have the presence of mind not to flip out when she did tell me, understanding the courage she had to muster, the fear she had to overcome to say it out loud.

Fear aside, for now it had become a normal state of being, I was always aware of it whirring away in the background like a familiar radio station. Neil would call and ask how she was and I would do my best not to worry him; I needed him to concentrate on his business and I would deal with things at home. The strain was phenomenal, coping with it on my own, wondering if what I was doing was the right thing or if I was making things worse. I had no one to ask and didn't really know how to find any information that would be helpful. Most things at the time were about the sufferers' perspective and that was no help to me at all. I had isolated myself to some extent. I didn't know where to ask for help but then I've never been good at asking for help, seeing it as a weakness, an admission that I couldn't cope, didn't have an answer. I've changed now; I had to, and when I did life became so much easier, much less complicated.

It seemed to me then that every decision regarding Nelly fell on my shoulders and if I chose the wrong one I was certain she would die, the family would fall apart and I would fall apart. Neither Neil nor Nick made me feel that the burden was mine alone, they were both strong and supportive but that's how I felt. It's interesting how much we look to mothers on how to deal with these things. I've since watched programmes on eating disorders. On the whole it's the mothers who are interviewed. Not many fathers make the screen; is that by choice or because they aren't asked? I don't know the answer to that. I've met fathers and partners at clinics and support meetings, some responded to my questionnaire which was a surprise to me but perhaps not to those in the medical profession. As a result I know that they care and worry just as much, blame themselves and feel utterly helpless. And it makes me wonder whether I took this stance by myself, shutting everyone else out. Such a bloody martyr, I can fix it, yes I can. But mostly I think it's down to being a parent, pure and simple. From the day our children are born we are there to soothe and comfort and we never stop wanting to do that, no matter how old our children are.

I know that all of this was a total puzzle to Neil and Nick, they were taking the lead from me and I had better know all the answers, hadn't I? It was like sitting in class at school, the teacher asking random students questions and I would sit there, sweat beading, in case they chose me and I got it wrong. Every day I was in that classroom, not knowing the answer.

I was determined to carry on as normal.

Chapter 10: Food, Glorious Food

One of my lowest moments was when Nick asked if it would be better if he and his wife didn't come over for meals for a while. I was devastated. Piece by piece the family life I had built was being taken apart.

I insisted that they did.

"If Nelly doesn't want to sit at the table, that's fine. She can load the dishwasher or watch TV, whatever she wants to do but we don't have a problem with food and we will carry on as we have always done."

I didn't consider their feelings, their discomfort and I regret that, but then I didn't consider anything other than keeping life as normal as possible when in fact it was anything but. But if I couldn't sit down to a meal and conversation with my kids what else was there? It was one of the few occasions we got together, time to talk, to discuss plans and dreams and support each other. Heaven knows what the atmosphere was like as I was oblivious to how anyone else was coping. Did they find the whole thing tortuous? I am afraid to ask in case it makes me go over and over how I could have done things differently but I can't change what I did do, only what I can do now.

I was so focused on having a life and if any family member asked my advice they got the answer that I thought best at the time. Would I do the same again? Probably. It was hard and I was bloody minded carrying on in the best British stiff upper lip tradition. It was hard for all of us. But, we kept on eating. It didn't help that my daughter was obsessed with food from one perspective while my son was passionate about it from another. Always adventurous, he was ever in search of new discoveries on the food front which led to a career as a food writer. So while he ate moss ice cream in Denmark and insects in China as part of his research, I was dealing with Nelly's obsession with food from the direct opposite. It became all about the food. I was dealing with the delicate balance of one child eating things that might make me feel sick and the other being coerced to eat and not be sick. I can laugh now, it seems so funny – but at the time, it was a bloody nightmare, trying to be a good mum and feeling pulled every which way in an attempt to encourage and support them both.

I drove Nelly to every clinic appointment, sitting in that small waiting room whiling away the time, listening to Ken Bruce on Radio 2. Sometimes I longed to be on the other side of the door, feeling sure that I would be able to help, that I would make this all happen faster if I was involved, that I could fix it, fix her, mend the parts that were broken. It took me a long time to learn that I couldn't do that and it was a painful, lonely lesson.

She has said since that this was probably a good thing as she might not have opened up so much in therapy, afraid of hurting me even more than she knew she was already. Eating disorders are about control and if I ever felt totally out of control then this was it. But by being excluded I was being subjected to another layer of control.

Nevertheless, I was determined that this eating disorder would not define my daughter, it would not define my family, and it most certainly would not define me. See, I told you I was naïve because even though I fought not to let that happen it did; you can't help but be defined by testing situations. I was so angry with everything, especially by the fact that at a time when I should be enjoying some semblance of stability my whole world seemed to be crumbling.

During our drives to and from the clinic I sought to learn more about her illness, about the things she needed to talk about. In the end it didn't matter. Getting well was what mattered, everything else was irrelevant, but my fear shot into overdrive when I learned about The Bitch.

Chapter 11: The Bitch

To conquer her eating disorder Nelly had to conquer 'The Bitch'. Let me explain.

The Bitch as we called her from then on was an entity, a voice, separate from her and yet part of her, and The Bitch had all the power in the relationship. We all have that critic to some degree, that inner voice that fills us with self-doubt. I wish mine was as cute as Jiminy Cricket but it isn't. It's the voice that tells me why bother, who cares, who do you think you are. Mine starts up every time I sit down to write and you may have read this far and wondered why I didn't take any notice and quit while I was ahead. Believe me, I've thought that many times but something inside me needs to get this story written. I have learned to tune this voice out, turn down the volume, ignore it and carry on. I have taught myself strategies to push through the noise. Shouldn't I be able to teach Nelly to do the same? If she had a voice surely it was her voice, her head, another critical part of her that she could choose to ignore? I had not realised how dominant the voice of the Bitch was. We called her the Bitch but others may have a different name – the Monster, the Dragon – they were all describing that same inner, dominant voice.

Nelly told me that The Bitch was her constant companion, one that she didn't know how to shake off. The bully she could not conquer. The Bitch told her constantly that she was worthless, a failure, a waste of space upon this earth. If she ate something she was rubbish, a flake, a wimp. If she was sick or ate little she was a success. It was so frightening to think that This

Bitch was real enough in her head to take control. I had a dilemma. How could I conquer something I could not see, that I couldn't hear? It wasn't like she had a friend I didn't want her hanging around with. There was no escape, no keeping her away from bad influences. This monster was telling her on a minute by minute basis that she was insignificant and was better off dead, that everyone would be happier without her causing problems and ruining their lives. At this point I became filled with utter dread. How could I manage this? I was a mum and I loved my daughter, I wasn't a therapist, a counsellor, a psychologist. I was way out of my depth. I couldn't hear what the voice was saying so I couldn't reason with it, couldn't reason with her. The Bitch had the loudest voice and it was with her constantly.

When she was at her lowest point, the voice persistent, I told her that the Bitch would never win, because I loved her more, my strength was endless and I would win no matter what; that I would be her strength when she couldn't find the wherewithal to fight.

As many parents and carers will tell you, the mental logistics or fighting an unseen foe is mentally as well as physically draining. Trying to keep one step ahead is nigh on impossible. You keep it to yourself because if you have never had experience of a mental health problem it's so hard to understand why people don't just pull themselves together and get on with life. If only it were so simple.

One Saturday night she came in, her face contorted in anguish, crying hysterically that she couldn't take any more and wanted to hurt herself, to end it all. It was 11.00pm on a Saturday night and I was alone in the house. I tried to comfort her but she was getting more and more desperate and so was I. I phoned the NHS helpline, I was at a loss as to what else to do. I know some people have had bad experiences with it but that night it was my lifeline. Someone took my call, talked me through what was happening and said someone else would call back in an hour and a half and if they didn't, to call again. I was terrified, how was I going to keep her calm for that amount of time? It was going to be a long night. Within forty-five minutes someone called again, not just someone but a doctor who specifically dealt with eating disorders. I passed the phone to Nelly and sat in the chair and waited. I had no idea what he said to her (there is a theme here – there always is, especially when they are over eighteen) but he obviously said exactly the right things as she became calmer and able to cope, and as a consequence I did too. And so there followed another night, lying half awake, listening for sounds in the house that might indicate she was up and about and possibly trying to harm herself. But we got through it.

There was also a period of disassociation. Nelly called in a panic. She had driven to a nearby town and couldn't remember how she had got there and was frightened. She had gone into a supermarket and been served by someone she knew from school. He had been concerned and came out to find her to check that she was OK. God bless that young man. She had been in some kind of trance and he had known her well enough to notice that something was wrong, not only that, but to check she was OK. Kindness indeed. She had other periods, with no recollection of going to places, how she got there, what she did. I became afraid of her driving alone, for her safety as well as for other road users. I don't know what triggered these episodes, only that it was all part of the bizarre process, stressful and frightening for both of us.

I had thought that once she got help at the clinic she would get better, in a gradual healing process but she became a whole lot worse, her behaviour more extreme before she found herself on a more upward trajectory. That wasn't to say that sometimes she slipped backwards but she didn't fall down so far each time. It was a zig-zag road to recovery and it would have helped to have been prepared for it. Not to have our hopes lifted then dashed time and time again.

So we blundered along, day by day, some days better than others. I dreaded anything that might trip her thoughts into a negative pattern, fearing that it would be the thing that made life not worth living. When we got news that her friend had been badly injured in Afghanistan I thought the time had come. Although surgeons fought to save his life he didn't make it. His mother was living through my worst nightmare and I thought I would be next. How selfish of me. How shameful.

Seeing his friends gather and support each other was bittersweet; how they shored each other up, helped where they could. The funeral would take place when she was on holiday with her boyfriend, his mum and his siblings. I already had concerns about her driving after discovering the periods of disassociation and a three-hour drive to Somerset was beyond her capability at that time. She wasn't safe and neither would anyone else be. I advised her not to go on the holiday but this only caused her more stress and she gradually worked herself into a state, mentally going round and round in circles. She would be letting people down. They were looking forward to it, as was she. She had to go – and I had to do something as I couldn't bear the stress of impending danger. I insisted that she would have to tell the clinic about these episodes and get some sensible advice as her insurance would not be valid. It was a total guess on my part but I didn't have time to find out if it was fact. She agreed and during her session I waited outside once more. A more senior therapist was notified and we had to go away for an hour and come back for an emergency appointment. We went to a cafe overlooking the sea, wild and untamed, the beach deserted. It felt hollow and empty. We ordered coffee and waited some more. We were getting to be experts at it.

It was an anxious wait, wondering what would they say; I was dreading her reaction. What if they said she couldn't drive? How could I stop her? She was an adult, I had no say in the matter, even when, day after day, I was living with this nightmare alongside her, I was actually powerless to do anything at all. I couldn't let her drive a car with passengers, fearing for their safety and hers as well as any other innocents it might affect. So, would I have to call the police, get her arrested? This is how my thoughts tumbled on, relentless, searching for solutions for things that might never happen but just in case.

Time up, we went back to the clinic and I sat waiting outside another closed door.

Towards the end of the meeting I was brought in and asked to express my concerns. As the discussion went on, strategies were put in place to protect her. If she was to go on holiday she would have to drive with someone who would keep talking to her, tell her to stop for a break at relevant points. After agreeing a strategy we left and I then had to go to her boyfriend's mum and explain the situation. I felt a bloody fool, telling her what needed to happen because my beautiful daughter was in a vulnerable place. She probably thought I was a raving lunatic and it was no wonder that my daughter was unhinged, what could you expect with a mother like that? But it had to be done and I became more and more shameless to keep her safe.

Although I felt weak and vulnerable, that I had lost my own inner compass, I had found an inner strength that galvanised me to protect my daughter. I did not understand the complexity of eating disorders before I was confronted with one. I had no idea of the intricacies and tortures of a sufferer's mental health. I thought it was life-threatening through starvation and damage to organs but I was more terrified that she would take her own life. I became a warrior mother, metaphorically standing in front of her to thwart harsh words, disapproving looks and ignorant comments that might make her worse. That one tiny thing that might tip her over the edge. Whereas, once I might have bitten my tongue to avoid causing conflict I now prepared myself to stand up for my daughter in a more vocal way than I had done previously. Before, I would have avoided conflict or embarrassing myself in any way, preferring to walk away. Now I found myself facing it head on – and if anyone dare challenge me – or my behaviour – I was ready to defend myself and stand my ground.

Chapter 12: Remembering is Reliving

Watching Nelly fade away was bad enough, grey skin, gaunt face. As I wrote this the remembrance of the Great War had begun (4 August 2014). On the BBC early morning news was the story of the Anderson family from Glasgow: a couple who had four sons, three lost to the war, one survived to die soon after at the age of twenty-one. How do you recover from that? Do you recover? How do you not drive yourself insane with worry while they are at risk and, God forbid, how do you cope when they are lost to you? Yet people cope with this every day of their lives to some degree or another. Most of the time we think our children are perfectly safe at school, work, going about their lives in relative comfort and safety, until some bolt from the blue turns everything upside down.

Millie became more of a comfort than ever, it's a wonder she wasn't squashed with all the tight hugs Nelly gave her. Oh, and she was indulged. Once, when Millie was ill, we googled how to look after her and finding that we should feed her plain chicken and rice went off to the supermarket and bought a whole chicken. We then poached it with a bowl of basmati rice and fed it to her over the next couple of days. She perked up good and proper after that and we congratulated ourselves on our new found veterinary skills.

She was always there, waiting on the rug at the front door when Nelly came in, then lying by her feet when she sat down. Dogs know, don't they, when someone is in need of comfort? Millie certainly did and her gentle presence soothed a lot of ills.

I look at photos of that time and Nelly appears ghostlike, gaunt cheeks, grey skin, a pale shadow when everyone else looks robust. It's almost as if she wasn't there, which many times she didn't want to be. The awkwardness is plain and looking at them fills me with pain at how fragile she was then, how fragile life was for us all.

Nelly was working for a PR company when she told us her problem was out of control. Ironically, it was a company that represented cooking equipment, a cosmic joke to be in a place where food and its preparation was ever present.

She went through quite a few jobs after leaving school. She would start well enough but leave abruptly when she couldn't cope with innuendo, sexual banter, the young men passing comment. She was never out of work for long but she couldn't seem to settle anywhere. She was forever running out of money and I could never understand why until I realised she would have periods when she spent most of it on food before binge eating then sicking it up. It was all or nothing, a life of extremes.

And she cooked, a lot, baking cakes and quiches, things stuffed full of calories. That's a common situation that those with eating disorders concentrate on – that although they won't eat they want to make sure everyone close to them does. It's so weird, this relationship to food, being around it and able to master not consuming it, a supreme act of willpower to be among the smells and aromas and yet never partake of it themselves.

I don't know if there's a western woman alive that doesn't know the calorific value of an apple, an egg or a slice of bread. It doesn't give us eating disorders. It was only when Nelly became ill that I realised that although the focus of control was around food it wasn't actually about the food. The food was a vehicle over which she could exact control as she couldn't control everything else. Controlling food made her feel safe and the more she exercised that control the more I lost it.

I developed an almost insatiable hunger. I began eating almost continuously, never feeling sated. I don't think I even ate because I was hungry, it was as if I was eating for two. If I ate I would keep her alive, I would keep her well. I wonder what other strange things I did unconsciously? I still haven't shifted that extra stone and am grateful now that it wasn't much more. I obsessed about food, making sure I still cooked as always but eating, snacking, comfort food. I can only think that adrenaline coursing around my system burned off many of the excess calories I consumed because theoretically I should be twice if not three times my size.

I've spoken to many parents who think that if they don't cook from scratch, that if they don't eat at the table together it will cause an eating disorder. I consider myself a fair cook, nothing fancy, just plain home cooking; we sat down at the table to eat as a family from when my children were tiny so it couldn't be down to that. My exercise was walking the dog, housework and gardening, nothing out of the ordinary. I never went to the gym and the only exercise I ever did on a regular basis was yoga, which was more about relaxation and inner mastery than size or shape. So looking back at my own example to her I couldn't find anything that I thought stood out as a trigger. Still, I was certain it was my fault, my neglect, my lack. But if it was then surely both of my children would suffer from eating disorders? Oh, if only I could have been so rational then.

I never obsessed over my appearance, some days I barely looked in the mirror but I didn't slob about either. Working mostly from home there didn't seem to be much point making too much effort. There were more pressing things to be getting on with than preening in a mirror. Conversely, I considered that this might have been the problem too – perhaps I should have spent more time on my appearance. If I had taken better care of myself, had regular manicures, gone on spa days, respected my body instead of taking it for granted then maybe she would have taken more care of herself, respected herself more, loved herself, had stronger self-worth. Always, always the constant guilt and self-blame; it had to be something I did or did not do that caused this. And there you have it. I realise it was all about me. I was the ultimate control freak, the power hungry mother.

How could anything happen to my children that was not of my doing? I feel so sad writing this now, pitiful creature. I thought I was a good, kind mother but it seems I was arrogant and pompous, not giving any credit to my children for their own will, their own personalities. I'm not being 'poor me' about it, just stating a fact from a new awareness of my own behaviour. Perhaps those fearful years of losing my home and stability left me in a permanent state of anxiety, so that I had to be strong and protect my family at all costs.

It is so much easier standing on the hill of hindsight,

looking back to see the past with more clarity, almost as if everything was inevitable given the circumstances. And yet my parents went through tumultuous times and we three girls didn't get eating disorders.

I sought help for myself, not the self-care of spa days but went for Cranio Sacral Therapy (CST). My aunt had been an alternative health practitioner when it was way off the scale of weirdness. She would give various healing treatments that helped me cope with stress but she lived in Lincolnshire and had passed away in 2008. I looked for someone close to where I lived and found a wonderful woman with whom I felt comfortable. My sessions were part talking therapy and part hands-on CST, although hands-on in the lightest sense. I took off my shoes, lay on the bed and she cradled my head, tilting it gently, realigning the energy. You may dismiss and ridicule any of these therapies but I think in any circumstances you should choose what is right for you and I would also say don't knock it until you've tried it. I shed many tears, talked of my greatest fear – that I would lose my child.

"And what if you do?" she asked one day

"It would be unbearable, I think I would die inside, I can't bear to think about the pain."

Yet people have to bear it. My own in-laws had borne it for years when they lost a child over fifty years ago. The therapist suggested that Nelly was a chrysalis, asleep in order to gain energy to spring forth as a butterfly. She had to go through the fire, the transformative process for herself, I could not do it for her. All her energy was being used for rebirth, for remerging as something quite beautiful. That one image helped me so much and I clung to it, that this process was something Nelly had to go through to emerge as her true self, brighter and more colourful instead of the grey, wishy-washy weak child she now was.

It's easier, with the passing of time, to reflect on my part in it all and my reactions. All the time second-guessing, wondering what would work, what might make it worse. I was in fact looking for a quick fix, I think we all are these days, a symptom of our culture. We want it now and we want it without much effort on our part. We want to pay £2 and win the lottery, we want a gastric band to lose weight, we think we will be more confident, more popular, more successful if we have the right haircut, perfect teeth, big boobs and the latest smartphone. It might be so for some people, winning the lottery would solve money problems but more than likely create many more. There is research to suggest that if you were happy before you won the lottery there's a good chance you'll be happier after you've won it, and if you were miserable before it won't make much difference.

I suppose it is attitude and temperament. Who knows for sure? All I wanted was a system, a fail-safe, step by step process that I could follow to make Nelly well. I simply wanted someone to tell me how to fix it. Well, there is no easy way as I soon discovered. It's a slow process, finding what works for you and your family. What worked one day might not work the next so you have to keep adapting. The thing is, no one has all the answers. It would be great to take a tablet and know it would all be better in the morning but that hasn't happened – not yet anyway.

Chapter 13: Labels

During one of my waiting room sessions at the outpatients clinic I was shocked to read one poster on the clinic wall - help for carers. I was a carer? It hadn't dawned on me that that was what I was, that this was my label. I was a mother doing what mothers do. Carer - the very word made me feel trapped, burdened, and I didn't want to feel like that. In that one instance I felt that this would go on forever. Part of me wanted to accept it, let go, fall into a safety net, and some other part of me would not admit that I needed help and support. I was strong, I could do this on my own. I saw this as my problem but perhaps a problem felt by others? I've never been very good at asking for help but part of that was shame, admitting that I was weak, that I didn't know how, I didn't have the answer. It meant that I had failed. I was tempted to go to the carers' group meetings that met once a month but each time I had something that clashed which meant I couldn't go. Would it have helped? I can tell you -Yes! Yes! Yes!

I've since been to lectures and meetings and it's such a relief to be in a room where you are not judged, where you don't have to explain anything, where people truly understand the horrible place you find yourself in. It is also refreshing to meet those wonderful young men and women who have been through recovery and out the other side of the darkness. From the moment I discovered my daughter's eating disorder I lived each minute in fear and belonging to a support group takes part of the fear away. Support is a wonderful thing and I'm sure if I had embraced it earlier it would have made things much more bearable.

Instead, solitary battling was wearing me down. I fell asleep exhausted and woke exhausted, fearful of what the day would bring. This constant fear paralysed me, affected every choice I made, everything I did on a daily basis. I was forever calculating the possible consequences of even the smallest of decisions – if I went out or wasn't there for her, that my mobile was always on and had a signal. I left it on the table in restaurants and would answer it immediately if I saw her name flash up.

It's glaringly obvious to me now how draining it was but also how fruitless. It achieved nothing and, if anything, kept me stuck in the middle of the vortex that I had found myself in when Nelly told me what was wrong. From the very first moment I was controlled by the possibility that she would die. That was my biggest mistake. It made me lose my objectivity over the situation, it clouded my thoughts, affected my judgement. I spent my time focused on Nelly or The Bitch – and what a waste of time and energy that was.

The thing is my story is not the darkest, there is light and shade, there is a happy ending. My daughter didn't end up in hospital on life support with damage to her internal organs, we didn't get divorced, family life didn't disintegrate. We were lucky, we fought hard not to and crucially, we got great help from the moment we sought it out. It wasn't anything we did or didn't do specifically, lots of it was simply being well placed to get the help we needed. But many parents do everything they can, as quickly as they can and are placed in an impossible situation when they still can't help their child recover.

I recently read *Into the Mourning Light* by Andrea Corrie, a mother's account of the grief she felt when losing her son who was walking home late at night. He fell into a canal and drowned. She writes of her son, of her grief, of other people's reactions and responses. What struck me was when she described how other people said that they didn't know how she could go on because they would not be able to, and she felt insulted. That they somehow implied that she couldn't have loved her son as much as they loved their children. That because she was still walking, still breathing, that her love was less. I wish I had read that before, I wish I could have somehow put it in perspective when I was dealing with Nelly's illness. It might have helped. But would I have been able to remember it when I was so gripped by fear? Unnecessary fear is debilitating, it serves no great purpose. Fear and worry drag you down, make you make the wrong choices or worse still, not choose at all. I realise that most of my life I have lived in fear, unwarranted or not, it doesn't matter.

I didn't lose my child and most likely you won't lose yours. If only I had not been so afraid, then perhaps I would have been able to be more objective and keep myself in better mental and physical health than I did. Perhaps. And then again, perhaps not. But I do know that once I stopped being afraid I was not only able to handle Nelly much better but also get back on track with living my own life to the full.

I think of the Eating Disorder as a bully, albeit one I couldn't see. How would you help your child deal with a flesh and blood bully? You wouldn't tell them to shrug it off and neither would you follow your child around twenty-four hours a day. Can you imagine the pressure someone with an eating disorder feels having that inner voice criticising them every minute? How tiring it is, how wearying? The last thing they need is you being the bully as well, telling them to eat, hovering over them as they take each mouthful; sitting there minute after minute, tense and expectant. It isn't going to work; put yourself in their shoes. However, as you tread that fine line between being firm and being a bully you can't let them do as they please and you need to set agreed boundaries. Once you stop panicking and imagining worse case scenarios you can gain a modicum of equilibrium and gain some ground.

Chapter 14: Turning Points

Nelly attended the clinic regularly and things seemed to be progressing nicely. She was working hard at the strategies they gave her and learning to cope with, and master, her mental health. I began to look forward with a hope I hadn't felt for months, which turned out to be short lived. It was the Sunday of August Bank Holiday, just after lunch. My stepson, Anthony, and his wife, Mandy, had been staying with us for the weekend and were about to set off for home as we, Neil and I, were to attend a surprise birthday party for a colleague that afternoon. Somehow, life had to progress, we had to keep being 'normal'. I desperately wanted to feel that I had a life to live and that by carrying on in this way I was setting an example to Nelly – but also showing her that her eating disorder was not ruining my life. I wanted to remove any added pressure from her to ease any guilt she might feel. My life had become so complicated, weighing up the effect of even the smallest of events.

We were relaxing, having a coffee before they left, when Nelly called, sobbing. I finally made out from her strangled words that her boyfriend had broken up with her and could I pick her up.

Panic; immediate panic. This was it. This was definitely it. Now we would tumble back down again, I just knew it. I asked Anthony to stay longer, collected Nelly and consoled her, finding out what had happened, calming her down, soothing her as always. Once she was calm and more resolved I left her with Anthony and Mandy, and Neil and I went to attend the surprise bit of the party. I compromised, trying to please everyone as always and feeling torn. And I hold myself entirely culpable that this people pleasing behaviour was not a good model for my daughter to follow and consequently contributed to my own mental health problems.

I arrived agitated, wishing I was at home, feeling trapped somewhere I hadn't wanted to be in the first place. Exchanging pleasantries to people I mostly didn't know was agony, all the while looking for an appropriate moment to escape. I couldn't get home fast enough. Forty minutes seemed like hours. Heaven knows what I looked like, high on drugs quite possibly, deranged probably but I was now past caring what other people thought any more.

I was convinced that this would be the tipping point; she would feel ugly and worthless as we all do when someone we love and care for does not return the feelings. How would I cope this time? My energy was depleted already, I wasn't certain I had the reserves I needed to support her through this but I knew that I would find them from somewhere. And do you know what? It turned out I didn't need them. This turned out to be an ending for her but also the brightest of new beginnings. I vividly remember her coming out of her bedroom on the following Tuesday morning and calling to me that something had clicked in her brain and she knew she would be alright. She had felt the physical click happen. I didn't question it I just hoped and prayed that it was right. And by and large it was. A few months later she met the wonderful young man who was to become her husband. Yes, I was afraid it was too soon, that she was rushing into things too fast but there was something so strong and solid about him that gave her renewed strength and confidence and I began, at last, to relax.

Things didn't improve overnight. It was still a long hard slog with two steps forward and three back but at least we were going forward. Gradually her visits to the clinic became less, and further apart. There were still relapses when she went into total meltdown but these periods were intermittent and she recovered more quickly from them. As things improved for her, I began to get my own life on a more even keel.

If I were to urge you to do one thing it would be to not give in to your darkest fears about your child, because all the things I was afraid of never happened, and all that wasted energy, that could have been used for a better cause, passed me by. Had I been able to stand back, to observe with a dispassionate eye, I would have not only helped her better but I would have been kinder to myself, a lot kinder. We've all heard the advice that if you are on a plane that gets into trouble you are told to put on your oxygen mask first before helping anyone else. That is the best advice I can give. Take care of yourself first, then you'll be strong enough to look after everyone else. Neglecting yourself, getting yourself tied in knots trying to save everyone else will very near kill you. When I talk to other parents whose children are suffering from eating disorders the first thing I want to tell them is to try and step out of the fire they find themselves in. Yes, I know, so much easier said than done but please try.

# # #

I often think that having Millie in our lives reflected so much of the journey we were going through with Nelly. I had to learn patience and realise that there would be setbacks – when I would be left with yellow stains on my cream carpet and poop in the hall. Progress would be made swiftly and then behaviours would regress and I would have to be consistent, reinforce the good behaviour, ignore the bad. I think that's good advice if you are trying to make progress in anything, even with yourself. I try not to be too hard when I slip back with things I am trying to master. I don't expect to turn things around so quickly any more.

There was a subtle but definite hierarchy between George and Millie. He would put up with so much of her puppy playfulness and then he would check her quickly and firmly and that would be the end of that. No going over things as humans do but a short reprimand and he would settle back down to snooze. I learned a lot from that too! You need to check the behaviour and forget about it, move on. Don't torture yourself trying to think what you could have done better. Leave it behind where it belongs.

When Nelly felt that click in her brain she really did enable herself to step away from the control of The Bitch. There were lapses, it was no miracle cleanse that fixed everything in an instant but it was most definitely a turning point.

Despite a few blips she and her new boyfriend grew closer. He came along at just the right time. He was a strong, secure young man, not a boy, and able to make Nelly feel safe. He did not play games with her feelings and was open and honest which was exactly what she needed to support her recovery.

I began to relax a little, not be so fearful now that she had Luke in her life. But if I had thought that life would become calmer, that I could restore my energies, I was very much mistaken.

In the January both my in-laws passed away within ten weeks of each other.

Their deaths, funerals and many other arrangements that come with such events involved long journeys north. Their belongings sorted, the house sold. It was a painful time, especially for Neil.

If that wasn't enough, at the beginning of June my father became ill, seriously so. We spent many months travelling to Lincolnshire to visit him in hospital and subsequently at home. The burden of care fell mostly on my mum and sisters and I felt torn that I wasn't there with him, or able to help them.

By October Nelly was pregnant. It wasn't what they had planned but they dealt with it admirably and it was quite possibly the best thing that could have happened to her. It was something to look forward to.

My father was in and out of hospital and died at home in the February of the following year. I wasn't there. We had visited a few days earlier and left on the Thursday because heavy snow was forecast. Dad had been alert, brighter than he had been for weeks. When I left that day I believed he had turned a corner and was going to get well. In the early hours of Sunday we got the call to tell us to get there as quick as we could but it was a five hour journey at best, and it had been snowing since Thursday morning. I received another call while we were driving to tell me he had died.

I went into total denial about it. This way of coping had served me well all my life but had reached a point where it was becoming dangerous to my own mental health and well-being. It was the beginning of my own slide into depression – not that I was aware of it at the time.

Nelly and Luke's daughter, Elsie, was born in the May. Nelly had pre-eclampsia during the latter stages of her pregnancy and her induced labour was long and painful. They were living with us at the time and I spent many, many hours holding Elsie, such a simple comfort but so valuable. I had been so devastated at losing my father that I blocked it out, easier to do when you live 300 miles away from your family. I could believe he was still alive, still at home with my mum. Eventually most of my days were spent in a chair nursing my granddaughter, soothing myself with this gift of new life – it quite possibly saved mine.

A few months later the three of them moved into their first home. Almost two years later Nelly gave birth to her son. Once again I was present in the delivery room and once again she had a long and difficult labour. The consultant came in many times to perform tests, and we all stared at the machine that was monitoring the baby's heartbeat. When Hadley was eventually born, the midwives and consultant left the room, and Luke went to tell Neil (who was in the waiting room) that mother and child were both safe. Nelly and I were talking and then there was a gush of liquid onto the floor.

"That's not wee, Mum," Nelly said. And it wasn't; blood was pouring from her. We rang the alarm and then the room was full once again with midwives and the consultant stitching her up, getting covered in blood in the process.

I finally arrived home at 6.00pm the following evening, exhausted and barely able to speak, had a bath and fell into a long deep sleep. I awoke the next morning, shattered, managed to stumble through the day and was glad to slump into an armchair that evening. I was finally beginning to unwind when Millie was sick on the lounge floor (this is the last time I have a cream carpet). I dragged myself to my feet and cleaned it up, cursing as I did so. It was getting late, it would soon be time for bed and oblivion and hopefully when I woke up I would have my energy restored. I later let Millie and George outside for a while, put them to bed and went upstairs myself.

In the morning Neil went down to make a tea and came straight back up saying there was something wrong with Millie.

"She was sick last night, she'll be OK. Probably ate something in the garden that she shouldn't."

"No, this is different," he said. "You need to come and look at her."

I was so naffed off, not only had I to be midwife support, but now I was to be the bloody vet. Begrudgingly I grabbed my dressing gown and trudged downstairs, muttering that I deserved a lie in, it was Saturday and I had earned it after all. But when I saw Millie I knew something was seriously wrong. She couldn't move her head, and there was only a mere flicker in her eyes when she looked at me. Her breathing was becoming quite shallow and she'd been sick and couldn't lift her head away from it. I pulled at her collar but she couldn't move herself. This was definitely something more than a sickness bug. I left Neil cradling her, hearing his words soothe her and went to find the vet's number.

I dialled only to get an answer machine and be given another number, all the time trying to quell my rising panic. I called it and spoke to the vet who said that they weren't open for another thirty minutes but to bring her in if we were worried. By the time I got back to Millie I knew she was dying. I couldn't move her, her body was a lead weight, her breathing shallow, her eyes losing their light. Neil was still stroking her, talking to her in a soft low voice, his tears falling onto her coat.

"She's dying, Neil." I sat by her and stroked her head, knowing it would be futile to even try to get her into the car. Her body barely moved with each exhalation.

"She can't be, she's too young." And she was, only four years old, but she was slipping away from us with each shallow breath.

"She is," I said flatly, barely a flicker of emotion let alone compassion any more. Everything I had grieved over, the thought of losing Nelly, of her losing her child, of losing my dad, it was all too much now. Millie breathed her last faint breath and a small puddle of watery blood came from her mouth. We put a large towel over her to keep her warm and sat with her until the end. In less than a minute she had left us and we sat with her, shocked that we could lose her so fast. We pulled the towel and covered her over, moved George into another part of the house.

I was beyond any emotion now, thinking only of the practicalities, where would we bury her, how would we tell the kids. I was most concerned about how Nelly would take it, that Millie had always been seen as the golden light that pulled her through the darkness and now she was gone. I knew she would be full of post pregnancy hormones but she had her son, she had her beautiful family. Perhaps Millie's work was over and now it was time for her to go. I tried out various platitudes in my head before telling her and this was the one that I thought would fit best.

We buried her in the garden, where four weeks later we would bury George beside her, both with their collars and name tags. It was months before I grieved for their deaths, my loss. Nothing compares to losing a child or a parent but months later the house felt empty. I came home and it was clean, not a trace of mud, no fur balls in the hall. It was immaculate, clean and quiet, oh so quiet.

You get a bit punch drunk eventually, quite oblivious of how hard you have been knocked about, used to carrying on regardless – and we did, so much worse had happened, so much we had survived, so much to be grateful for. All these other life events were put into perspective. Losing my dad had been the worst thing; I had gone into a denial that eventually found me in therapy myself. Compared to losing my dad I could put losing my dog into a different perspective. I was sad to lose her but gosh, I could so easily have lost so much more.

I was tired beyond words, beyond thinking, days, drifted one into another. Food tasted of nothing, I no longer looked forward to cooking or eating. I didn't sleep, ridiculous empty thoughts kept me awake, things that didn't matter. Everything seemed pointless and too much effort. The doctor suggested that I might be depressed and referred me for therapy which, quite honestly, gave me back my life. I couldn't have gone on as I was; existing instead of living. Added to that, I hated coming home to an empty house, missed walking on the common at the bottom of the garden. I could have gone walking on my own but it wasn't the same. After four months I began searching the internet for dogs: smaller dogs, less energetic dogs and still went for a springer spaniel. I am nothing if not a glutton for punishment. By the time August came around we had a puppy, Harry, another springer who has chewed numerous socks and munched away at the skirting board. He lies at my feet while I type away, and gas emissions that hugely raise his carbon footprint aside, he is a wonderful companion. Where Millie healed Nelly, Harry has healed me. I get out walking whatever the weather, I am never fully alone and there is always someone at home waiting for my return. Exercise and fresh air have renewed my vigour and energy for life. And if you're still in doubt, get a dog; I reckon a dog will get you through anything.

Chapter 15: Afterwards and After Words

There are lots of times I've wondered whether I should keep writing this book. After all, maybe my child wasn't ill enough for me to consider myself worthy of contributing in any way; she wasn't hospitalised, wasn't drip fed or sectioned. More rationally I think that it didn't matter how ill she was, what mattered was that every day I thought I would lose her – either by slow starvation, her organs slowly grinding to a halt, or from jumping off a bridge into traffic, or taking too many pills. Then I might read an article about kids, very young kids of three or four, with dreadful disabilities or life limiting diseases. How could I compare my worry and fear with the parents of those children? And that is always the dilemma. No one inflicts cancer on themselves whereas on the surface it seems that anorexics and bulimics self-inflict their pain.

In the end it's all about measurement and you don't need scales to do that. We can measure ourselves against anyone we choose and fall short in some way or another. The trick is to stop comparing but how do you do that with any sort of consistency? Advertising and marketing makes us all too aware of what we don't have, that is their purpose after all and how can we avoid it?

It wasn't too long before I realised that I was playing the measurement game myself. I'm not good enough, pretty enough, clever enough. If my child fails or falls ill it is my fault, down to my failings as a mother. I'm not feeling sorry for myself here, it's just a fact, the thing I do, the thing so many of us do. It's all about self-worth isn't it? It's about valuing ourselves as we are, parent or child. I see many girls and boys, hear so many stories of children and grandchildren abusing themselves because they don't feel good about themselves in some way and although we ourselves may have felt this way I don't think the pressures were the same. The society we live in, of quick fixes and instant access has exacerbated things to such an extent that we are leading young people into a trap. We live an 'on demand' life, watch what we want when we want to, fashion changes erratically, cheap clothes encourage excess; expectations are high and fulfilment is low. There seem to be little or no boundaries, magazines are full of diets and photos of celebrities caught unawares looking, heaven forbid, normal, tired and weary, stressed. Captured wearing comfortable clothes and no make-up it seems to be a sin to relax and be at home in ourselves and in our skins, they are scrutinised and criticised to make us feel better in comparison. Images like this, pressures like this don't cause eating disorders but they don't help.

I am totally aware that this illness had as much a hold over me as it did Nelly. Trying to get her well consumed me as well as her. Ironic that I use the word consumed but apt, for it's like being devoured from the inside out.

Only recently have I been able to be in a place where I can actually take charge of my own eating patterns and bring my weight and eating back into control – and yet it's not control, it is choice. I am choosing to eat well. I am choosing not to overeat. Now that I am no longer in the thrall of the eating disorder I can see how I increased my portion size, eating far too many roast potatoes, having seconds, buying a pack of two custard tarts and eating both in one sitting. When stressed I craved food, comfort food, as I had never done before. I hope to continue being conscious of my eating. Again, it is a fine balance of being aware and not overly aware. Of choosing nourishing food over empty calories, of avoiding the sugar high that makes you feel better for a while and then slump in a chair for hours on end, lacking energy and inclination to do anything at all. I was also afraid that, if I started watching what I ate to lose the weight that I had gained, Nelly would notice and comment and that would immediately trigger the guilt. So I remained overweight because it was safe to be so. It took me a long time to detach myself from my child and start to take care of myself.

The more parents I talk to the more I realise how we are all sucked in by the eating disorder. It's like getting stuck in a glue, unable to pull yourself entirely free, the residue hard to remove entirely. It's so hard to reach a perspective on the situation to get an overview, panic draws you in and tangles you in weeds and tendrils that pull you back and keep you stuck. Once you can detach yourself though, things start to improve.

The majority of people align eating disorders with images of painfully thin young girls. I know that men and boys get eating disorders too but if you ask someone with no experience of eating disorders they will conjure up this stereotype, the gaunt hollow eyed, hollow cheeked child-woman. This is dangerous in itself because it leads one to dismiss all other options, all other signs and behaviours that signal there is a problem. You don't have to be seriously underweight to have an eating disorder. You can be overweight, you can be a perfectly balanced weight or your weight can fluctuate and you can still have an eating disorder. And because eating disorders are mental health problems they can go undetected and unsupported for a long time. If a person is skeletal (when previously they were not) we can hazard a guess that something is wrong even if we are not sure what it is. The association with dying of starvation, images in our memory of concentration camps are discomforting and we either want to look away or stare in disbelief. Yet, when someone is extremely overweight we want to look and stare because we can't believe that either. We are fascinated by how they function. It's as well to remember that eating disorders are a mental condition with odd behaviours and a tendency to suicidal thoughts, self-loathing and problems with body image.

Since Nelly became ill I became obsessed with the programme *Supersize vs Superskinny* because there was always an emotional problem at the seat of it. The same with hoarders and yet we dismiss that as odd, freaky, strange, but at some time all those people have been hurt and have been unable to deal with that hurt for one reason or another.

I'm now able to have photos of my dad around my home, listen to music he enjoyed, watch films that I had once loved watching with him by my side. Little things perhaps, but today I can look at them and smile whereas before it only made me sad and tearful, the pain unbearable. Today I can count myself lucky that I have those wonderful memories for they enable me to keep my dad close to my heart. Today I can appreciate my inner strength that got me through this challenge. Instead of thinking that everything I did was wrong I realise that these were my survival tactics, my coping mechanisms. And thanks to good help and support from family, friends, doctors and counsellors and therapists, both regular and alternative, I have come through the other side. I can recognise my strength and bloody mindedness and use it as an asset now. The realisation that it is an asset rather than a drawback has enhanced my confidence. How we view things is paramount. We are so used to berating ourselves, putting ourselves down, beating ourselves for not being good enough. We don't stop and think how wonderful we are, so why should our children think anything other than this about themselves when we set such a bad example. It's so easy to think you are failing at every turn when in fact you are almost certainly doing better than you think you are.

I am still angry at the loss of precious time. Quite possibly more angry now than I was when she was really ill. I was too frightened to be angry then. I am also angry for the loss of the person I was then but am at peace with the person I am now. I have moved on. Nelly is angry on occasion and she can use that energy to transform herself. Piecing things together is helping her make sense of the last few years and I know she will go forward now.

I almost lost my child and I only grieved for her when I started to get her back again, in sheer relief. I will always remember the terrible times but I am not haunted by them. It is memory, it is recall, but it has no hold on me any more. It feels great to be free at last.

I'm not certain you can stop your child getting an eating disorder; any more than you can stop them getting any mental health condition – or getting attracted to drink, drugs, smoking, or anything else that a parent worries about as their child grows up and away from them. Early intervention has proved to be an asset and I would urge you to get help as soon as you can. Don't be fobbed off, listen to your instincts, don't ignore them. If you don't get help quickly this could go on for years – it frequently does.

Part Two

Practicalities

Chapter 16: It's Not all About the Food

The NHS has seen a 66 per cent rise in hospital admissions in the last ten years.

There are many reasons people develop eating disorders and some of them are as follows:

- A build-up of pressures and anxiety over time
- Psychological genetic predisposition
- Environmental, social and psychological factors
- Contributing factors include bullying, dieting, sports size or job demanding thinness – jockey, model, wrestler, etc.
- Sexuality
- Living in a culture fixated on diets (physical appearance)
- Expectations of girls
- Identity, confidence, debt, expectation

It can be a combination and culmination of all of the above. Research continues and you can find out more by checking the B-eat website for the latest on how best to deal with an eating disorder. *www.b-eat.co.uk*

In the course of writing this book I contacted parents, some face to face, others by phone, many others by asking them to complete a questionnaire that I circulated at Kimmeridge Court in Poole and through B-eat, the national eating disorders charity. I am grateful to those parents who gave their time to answer my questions and share their experiences with me. Talking to them made me feel more sane, less guilty, less stupid. Many of their responses are included throughout this section. They remain anonymous but give an insight into the differing but common experience.

'When you think there may be a problem there probably is – confront the situation early and look for help as soon as possible. I am very glad I got help just over a year in as we have been told the longer it is left the harder it is to deal with so I would always recommend be proactive and don't be afraid to look the problem in the face and get on with helping the person get over it.'

What to look for
Hindsight is most definitely a wonderful thing. Until Nelly told me she had an eating disorder I didn't have a clue. As I've said before, she always loved her food. I had never worried about eating problems because I just didn't think she was the type – if there is a type. I wasn't in denial because I had simply dismissed it as ridiculous. When I spoke to other parents I understood that their children are as different as we are – and yet the same – there is no type.

'(I) started off thinking it was a phase – she always put weight back on when at home from uni but then when she got glandular fever and depression and lost more weight I was hoping it was that and not an eating disorder but at the back of my mind I had begun to consider anorexia.'

Trust your gut instinct. Like anyone with a mental health problem they are very good putting on a front of all being well. They may well display a reluctance to answer any of your questions to prevent you delving deeper but if you think something is wrong... it usually is.

> *'I did not realise she was not eating. But her mood was awful and she was refusing to go to school. We knew something was wrong but didn't know what.'*

So I had a stroppy adolescent, who doesn't? One parent I spoke to said she couldn't say that her daughter was a sweet compliant child before the eating disorder took hold because she wasn't, she was confrontational before that but now even more so.

Prepare to be manipulated because make no mistake, you will be. Anyone with a secret, no matter what that secret is, does not want to be found out and so they will go to any lengths not to be discovered. Their excuses and explanations will be so plausible that you will, by turns, think you are mistaken, jumping to conclusions, interfering or totally insane to think such things – how could you misjudge your darling child, how could you be so cheap, nasty and downright nosey.

'We were unaware of the complexity of anorexia and how this illness had taken over our daughter. When we saw that she was losing weight and we questioned her, we believed what she told us as she had never been a liar before and we didn't know that lying and deceit was a big part of her world at the time.'

Self-harm is common, cutting is common, any form of self-abuse goes hand in hand with eating disorders. Be on your guard to the signs, forewarned is forearmed. Again, get help as soon as you suspect there is a problem – I cannot repeat often enough – **this is a mental health issue!**

The best advice I could give you would not to be afraid. Fear ties you in knots that are hard to untangle.

'(I was) shocked at how serious the situation was – admission the next day was scary and it all happened so quickly. I felt worried and scared for my daughter's health and really I guess a bit disappointed that she had an eating disorder – there is still a lot of taboo about EDs.'

When you first find out you might become weakened with shock. It is so easy to become trapped in a vicious circle of doubt and fear which, try as you might, you can't pull yourself away from. You need to step out of it somehow. I know it's not easy, for you are blinded by sheer panic or bewilderment. I can only liken it to being in another country where you don't know the language or the custom and every word can offend or can have the reverse effect of what you expect. It's a steep hill to climb and you soon learn the phrases to avoid.

> *'...it was very difficult to deal with on a daily basis – to see your daughter crying and be unable to help her. We felt impotent.'*

I am therefore not stating that my experience was worse or better than anyone else's. Parents feel helpless, angry, sad, a whole spectrum of emotions being in this situation and, although there are differences, there are many things that are the same. It's not about who is the most ill, who is suffering the most, it's not a competition! It's important not to fall into the trap of thinking your child is not thin enough or ill enough, it's not about the outward appearance so much as the inner turmoil. The longer you leave it the longer it may take your child to recover. Please, please, get help as soon as you can. Be proactive from the beginning.

Common Signs to Look For

Not eating – (of course) – moving food around the plate
as opposed to eating it
Eating in secret
Eating 'safe' foods
Always on different diets
Food rituals – has to be prepared in a specific manner
or eaten on a certain type of plate
Cutting food into small pieces
Cooking for others but not eating themselves
Fear of eating in public
Saying they've eaten elsewhere
Going to the bathroom immediately after eating
Large amounts of food disappearing in a short amount
of time
Rapid loss of body weight
Over exercising
Going for long walks
Cleaning the bathroom – evidence
Wearing baggy clothes
Distorted self image
Irritability   Anxiety
Mood swings
Feeling life is out of control
Dental problems caused by vomiting all the time
Cuts and grazes on knuckles when they have made
themselves sick
Getting through lots of mouthwash and Tic Tac mints
(low calorie option to hide vomit breath)
Hair loss, dull hair, grey skin
Constantly feeling cold
More body hair (body's defence to keep warm)

How did you feel when you first found out?

'Shock despair, disbelief. Our world totally shut down and we felt helpless beyond compare.'

'My first reaction? – I'll fix this – before it goes any further. I knew all about anorexia (I'm a nurse) and some treatment strategies. I put this all down to a phase that my daughter was going through. Meanwhile, I discussed it with my husband, my mum, my closest friends and everyone agreed that she had lost weight, but no one really considered it a problem then. Was I making too much of it?'

'Relieved in a way that my suspicions had been confirmed as she had been to the doctor several times with glandular fever and depression and been weighed but it had not been picked up. I also felt relieved that she was at last getting the help she needed.'

'Shock, massive guilt, bewildered and scared. I went into autopilot. The hospital did not have a clue how to deal with someone with an ED.'

'Astonishment – of all our children we thought she would be the one to adapt the best to adult life, popular at school academically fantastic, and confident socially.'

Chapter 17: Myths

That it's entirely about food

> *'Once transferred to the specialist ED unit, one doctor suggested that it was a severe anxiety disorder rather than a full blown ED. For some bizarre reason that made me feel better – only months later did I realise how closely connected the two disorders are. She is now labelled as having anorexia.'*

That a good meal will fix it

> *'The relationship with my husband has grown stronger – we are both fighting the same thing. The relationship with my sister, mother, stepfather, aunts and uncles suffered greatly as they couldn't understand the illness and why (she) had become our priority in an overwhelming sort of way. Her grandmother's idea of solving the problem was to bake a huge chocolate cake.'*

That they are attention seeking

> *'After much soul-searching we let her go on holiday as we figured if she was drinking loads, she might start eating burgers and stuff and kick-start her eating again. After two days abroad her friends called me to ask me to get her home: she was self-harming, hadn't eaten in two days and was drinking excessively. We got her home on a flight that night and took her to the doctor the next day who diagnosed anorexia and told her to go home and eat three good meals a day!! If only*

it were that simple. Her reply? She said she couldn't eat today as she had eaten last week.'

That they are in control

'The defining moment was on my birthday actually. I found my daughter crying, really sobbing, in the kitchen. I had told her it was time for a snack (my mini food plan in action!) and she told me that she was so frightened because she couldn't actually eat it. She couldn't swallow it. She admitted then that it had taken over and she couldn't control it any more. Was it a relief? Only that now I could get some help.
I think I felt sick with worry from that day in September until around Christmas!'

'She had been ill from the age of seven or eight which was later diagnosed as cyclical vomiting syndrome. So had been ill for some time which has affected her gaining weight and eating anyway. By the time the ED was diagnosed at age twelve the cyclical vomiting had faded away. Who knows whether it was always an ED or something that had developed out of the cyclical vomiting syndrome? Either way she has not been properly well since about seven years old.'

'The worst memory was when we went for our first appointment and I then realised how very underweight she had become. What sort of mother was I? (68 per cent weight for height.)

*She would have been admitted but for her age.
No school and a wheelchair to mobilise. How
did this happen? She was racing last weekend!
I cannot describe how guilty I felt. Why
hadn't I gone for help sooner?'*

Chapter 18: Classifications of Eating Disorders

In the effort to keep things as simple as possible what follows is the briefest description of eating disorders. There are a multitude of subtleties in symptoms but to give you an overview they are as follows:

Anorexia
Anorexia as a serious mental health condition whereby people restrict their weight in an effort to be as thin as possible. To do this they will severely reduce their food intake, and/or make themselves vomit and may also exercise excessively. They have poor body image and think they are fat when they are thin.

Bulimia
A mental health condition. Sufferers restrict their food intake then binge and purge making themselves vomit. They may also use an excessive amount of laxatives. Again, poor body image, low self-esteem.

Atypical – or Eating Disorder Not Otherwise Specified (EDNOS)
An eating disorder will be described in this way when it does not meet the specified criteria for either anorexia or bulimia – they may have characteristics of some but not all or may move between one condition and the other. It possesses all the anxieties related to other eating disorders and is just as distressing.

At the risk of being repetitive, it's a mental health problem, doesn't matter if your child's not at death's door, weighs more than six stone or is not so weak that they can't stand. Get help as soon as you find out that your child has an eating disorder or you think there is a problem. Getting help fast has shown to create faster recovery times.

Orthorexia
Although not officially classed as an eating disorder, orthorexics have problems with food, having an 'unhealthy' attitude to healthy eating. It's not about eating less or weighing less, it's about wellness and purity of food taken to extremes; orthorexics eating only what they consider 'clean' food, resisting temptation, and planning their eating with precision. There then begins the cycle of punishment if they eat 'bad' food and a feeling of euphoria when they continue with their 'healthy' eating.

You can find out more at **www.orthorexia.com**

As I stated at the very beginning of this book, I am not an expert but common sense tells me that there will be an explosion in orthorexia in the next few years. There is so much media exposure of the latest celebrity diet – no sugar, no carbs, no gluten, and so on. I am tired of reading magazines containing recipes from the latest 'healthy' cookbook, written by shiny, lean young women with perfect, even teeth – give me Mary Berry every time. Life is about balance and enjoyment – why do we have to keep punishing ourselves? What are we teaching our young people about life? Excess and extremes are bad for anyone long term. We need to seek out balance even if we don't always maintain it. Yes, we need to eat well but a little indulgence now and again is perfectly acceptable and hopefully, enjoyable.

Body Dysmorphic Disorder

An anxiety disorder related to body image with its own obsessive behaviours. It may seem, on the surface, to be due to a lack of confidence or shyness. Beware, this is not vanity, this is more extreme. Almost all of us from time to time will be dissatisfied with our appearance. I know I was always unhappy about my crooked nose, my huge calves, to name but two things – but I did not suffer from dysmorphia. It might have made me self-conscious but it didn't stop me doing things, it did not disrupt my life in any great way. You can't heal this with a few kind words about how beautiful they are, they only see their imperfections. If you are worried about your child, don't be dismissive, it may well lead to more serious problems.

Society appears to focus on perfection in all things. I believe this has become worse with social media which young people in particular are more exposed to. Mostly people share the best of their lives, not the worst, and this can give a warped version of reality. The grass can certainly seem greener when put through the filter of Instagram and Facebook. More insidiously, the undercurrents of perfection are everywhere – even down to supermarkets not stocking 'ugly' vegetables. Forget the nourishment it offers, if it doesn't look perfect it doesn't make the grade then it won't make the shelves. What kind of message is that giving?

Chapter 19: Getting Help and Support for your Child

Your local Surgery or Medical Practice

Hopefully you will get good support from your doctors' surgery. This was my first port of call. I had been to the surgery many times with my daughter wondering what was wrong, why she was so grey and lethargic. They referred us to specialists who could find nothing wrong and I didn't for one minute think she had an eating disorder. I made assumptions – don't make the same mistake.

> *'Now I look back – I was obviously in denial as I didn't want to admit that this was too huge an issue for me to solve. I couldn't make her better. I felt that I was letting her down, but I was out of my depth. However, even in the early stages of treatment, I still felt that she had merely gone down the wrong path and she didn't really have an Eating Disorder!'*

On reflection I think perhaps I missed so many signs but because she had always been such a good eater I never thought it was a problem. I was missing the point because I wasn't looking for a mental health issue at all. Once she admitted the eating disorder to me I was able to get direction and thus find a way forward.

> *'Our first port of call was the mental health team… (useless). They were planning on monthly appointments of an hour at a time. After making myself heard (!) this was increased to more regular meetings but they*

*wouldn't admit her to hospital as she wasn't
small enough (which they told her to her face!
Idiots) and so tried to manage her in the
community. Of course, she tried and
succeeded losing more weight and was
eventually admitted to Addenbrooke's which
was her aim at this point. She was an
inpatient for five months.'*

Because my daughter was over eighteen the medical
profession were not able to speak to me without her
permission. (However, even if your child is under
eighteen you can still be excluded from parts of their
treatment.) I made the call (at Nelly's request) because
she couldn't find the courage and passed the phone to
her. She spoke to the doctor and relayed what was said
to me. I went with her to appointments and sat outside.
She was referred to the mental health assessment clinic
in a nearby town. We didn't have to wait long and I
dread to think what would have happened if we had.
Those few days waiting for her appointment were
fraught with stress and anxiety but at least we were
being taken seriously. I didn't have to fight for second
opinions – ever. No one told her to go home and get a
good meal inside her, she was taken seriously from the
first instance. We were extremely fortunate.

*'We had to battle at every step of the way.
Nothing was offered. We had to beg, plead,
shout, scream and refuse to leave
appointments until we got what we wanted. I
always apologised afterwards for shouting
though. I am not a volatile person – just a
desperate one.'*

*'Our GP was clearly inexperienced in the area
of anorexia and dealing with young girls. He
tried to give our daughter a 'chummy'
talking-to. When I explained about her limited
diet and vigorous athletics training, he
suggested she eat a Mars bar before going
running! He didn't think that she needed to
stop exercising and he didn't weigh her.
I had to ask for a referral to CAMHS* myself.'
*CAMHS – Child and Adolescent Mental
Health Services – a service to specifically
support those under eighteen with mental
health problems.*

Psychological/ Mental Health Assessment
Your child will be assessed and practitioners will
decide the next steps of treatment. In our case it was a
referral to the Eating Disorders clinic. If they are over
eighteen it's up to your child to say whether you come
into the discussion or not. I didn't as I respected her
privacy and also didn't think I was allowed to but
looking back I wonder if that was the best thing to do.
If she had been under eighteen I would have insisted.
Respecting her privacy throughout might have been the
wrong thing to do. I didn't even ask!

As part of the treatment your child will receive
therapy and you may also be offered it as part of their
treatment, both as a family and as an individual. This
differs from service to service, private to NHS, area to
area and also budget restraints. But as you are dealing
with the problem on a daily basis it stands to reason
that getting the whole family involved makes them
better placed to help the child recover.

'She dealt with it herself...didn't want us to interfere...is very strong minded...said she would sort herself out...to be fair to her, she seems to have conquered most of her demons.'

I think Nelly had a hard time becoming an adult and taking too much control from her would have been to her detriment. It's always, always about the control and we parents walk a fine line over whether to intervene or not. It was a balance of walking tentatively, asking myself questions, working out possible scenarios and possible reactions to what I could do. Mental gymnastics on a minute by minute basis was exhausting. I was endlessly anticipating what her reactions would be and trying to think of a way to either deflect or support her. My daughter was over eighteen. Under eighteen I would have taken control, no doubt about it. But that may have been the worst thing I could have done. However, I recently spoke to a parent whose child insisted the parent not be allowed in the room and the child in question was under sixteen. It all very much depends on so many factors; you, your child, the medical professionals involved and their procedure and protocol. Even so, I would urge you to be proactive as opposed to passive.

'I would not collude with the illness which I know now I did do. I would not have involved myself so much as I did. It is easy to become involved in a symbiotic relationship which can be fatal for both mother and daughter. When you are asked by a consultant psychiatrist whether you just want them to give palliative care to your child you learn a lot about what

you would have done differently.'

In each instance you have to make a decision based on your knowledge of your child and the situation you find yourself in with the medical profession. At all times seek a range of advice and opinion before you make your decision.

> *'...I fought, shouted, begged and pleaded with people to get her help and gradually it appeared. I had never heard of B-eat before this illness. Initially we felt very alone and struggled, but after a while, she got help.'*

Referral to specialist or specialist unit Mental Health Clinic

My daughter was only ever an outpatient. Many times I wanted her to be an inpatient because I felt that at least I would know she was safe and there would quite possibly be a sense of relief, that someone else was responsible for her so that I could have a break. I barely slept, never relaxed until she was in the house, and even then if she was alone, wondered if I would wake and find her dead. I was a little less tense when I knew she was with either her boyfriend or friends. Knowing she was with someone made it somewhat easier.

Outpatient

This treatment could be clinic appointments once or twice a week depending on the severity of the mental health problem. At the moment budgets are tight and the numbers of sufferers continue to grow. In light of this, the frequency of outpatient visits could reduce – and the damage caused by EDs and mental health disorders could increase.

Inpatient
Your child is admitted to hospital or specialist unit based on the severity of case. Most usually this is when they have reached a specified low body weight and they will stay in until body weight is increased to a specific ratio. Sadly, it may also be dependent on what resources are available in your area. There may not be specialist facilities to hand and therefore your child may be admitted further away from home. This is another pressure you don't need, time travelling, time off work and the additional expense that ensues. However, whatever it takes to get your child well is worth it in the end.

> *'As an inpatient my daughter had access 24/7 to a range of services – psychiatry, psychology, dietician, OTs, hospital, school, support workers, etc. but once discharged, it became harder to access what she needed to keep moving forward with her recovery. We had one hour per week with a CAMHS psychiatrist and one hour a week for therapy work with a psychologist. No access to a dietician or any other support. Hardly surprising then that my daughter relapsed five weeks later where she became really poorly and was admitted to the general ward again for 2.5 weeks. She had lost all the weight gained in the nine months in the ED unit within five weeks, in addition had caught a stomach bug and then became very poorly. Heart was struggling with drastic weight loss*

in such a short time span. Was admitted on bed rest. After discharge we have been battling ever since and now she has been reassessed by ED unit and is now on the waiting list for readmission. There are simply not adequate services within the community for this type of condition.'

Help for Under 18s
Child and Adolescent Mental Health Services (CAMHS)

CAMHS is the term used for the wide range of services that help children with their emotional or behavioural well-being. A child will be under this treatment programme or department and transition to the adult service follows at sixteen or eighteen, depending on area. Speaking to other parents, this is where everything seems to fall apart. The transition is rarely smooth or adequately linked, and the process is disrupting if you have to start the whole admission process again from scratch.

The professionals your child comes into contact with may include many or all of the categories listed below:

- Psychologist
- Psychotherapist
- Family Therapist
- Child and Adolescent Therapist
- Nurses
- Social Worker

They may have individual therapy, sessions with one parent or as a whole family.

They will be given a treatment plan that will cover the process of care to get them well again.

> *'YPEDs (Young People's Eating Disorder Service) came every day. They took her blood pressure – heart rate, blood samples, weighed her, and left.'*

Help is patchy at best, dependent on where you live in the country and facilities (and budgets) available.

> *'(There was a) nine month waiting list for counselling with CAMHS which wasn't worth waiting for.'*

Please persevere to get the help you need. People with eating disorders, particularly anorexia, are high risk. They have the highest mortality rate of any psychiatric illness.

> *'CAMHS were brilliant at supporting us and referred my daughter within hours of meeting with us. It was a relief (after the GP being quite dismissive). The referral took two weeks to reach them due to the GP sending it to the wrong place. Very frustrating.'*

> *'I googled the YPEDS team following a chat with our daughter's Head of House. She was brilliant as she had experience of eating disorders with past pupils. I can't thank her enough.'*

Maudsley Approach

This is a family based treatment of adolescent anorexia for those under eighteen.

It consists of intensive outpatient treatment where parents play a positive and active role.

The treatment process has three phases:
i) Weight restoration
ii) Returning control over eating to the adolescent
iii) Establishing healthy adolescent identity

Refer to the website for more information and case studies **Maudsleyparents.org/whatismaudsley.html**

> '...my physio, who is also a good friend, had given me the number of the Maudsley Counsellor in our area a while ago, after she had seen how much weight my daughter had lost.'

National Institute for Health and Care Excellence (NICE)

For an overview of good practice you can check out the treatment guidelines for eating disorders.
https://www.nice.org.uk/guidance/cg9

"For all eating disorders: Family members, including siblings, should normally be included in the treatment of children and adolescents with eating disorders. Interventions may include sharing of information, advice on behavioural management and facilitating communication."

https://www.nice.org.uk/guidance/cg9/chapter/key-priorities-for-implementation

In my opinion, and I stress it is only my opinion, I think it's important that all close family members are involved because when someone has an eating disorder it affects the whole family whether you like it or not. Having guidance on how best to deal with day to day living would have given me great strength. To have affirmation of what I was doing right and what I could improve on would have helped enormously and given me greater confidence on a daily basis.

Sometimes the help will be forthcoming and other times you will have to fight tooth and nail to get the help you need for your child. I've tried to give a balanced view of parents' responses but sadly most felt unsupported and had to battle for help as you can see from responses below. If you are fortunate enough to have private health insurance you may fare better. It may also be that those parents who responded were more angry at lack of care and those who received good care didn't look back. As for my experience, I cannot thank the staff of the NHS enough for the brilliant care and support we received.

> 'She was immediately admitted onto a general paediatric ward and then transferred to the specialist ED unit, so was aware from the beginning that help was available. Problems really started when she was discharged – severe lack of services in the community.'

> 'The doctor took no action even though it was clear my daughter had lost weight and was weighed twice when she was being treated for depression.'

'My wife managed to get her to the doctors but without any success. She was told our daughter would grow out of it and not to worry!'

'I felt they were only concerned about medical side and basically I was left every day with a starving monster (she was so angry and I felt I didn't know her any more).'

'After discharge very limited. No 24/7 support like was available at the ED unit. Very much left to get on with it. The two hours a week we have been given via CAMHS have been excellent in terms of quality but in terms of quantity nowhere near enough (especially when first discharged). The lack of a dietician had had a huge impact on my daughter's recovery and subsequent relapses.'

Chapter 20: Getting Help and Support for Yourself

> *'I took six months off work to care for my daughter and felt that I did it all alone. K came to the rescue eventually and was great. She helped me to stop blaming myself.'*

When you are a carer you also need to be cared for and if there is no one around to do that for you, you must learn to do it for yourself. In fact, even if there is someone around to care for you THEN you most definitely need to learn how to be kind to yourself. Don't lose yourself in the circus that comes with an eating disorder. Caring for someone on this emotional level is draining, it becomes hard to concentrate, hard to remember what to do for yourself to relax and increase your ability to cope with stress.

> *'My daughter refused to have anyone in the house to visit – I couldn't go out as she would threaten to harm herself if I left her alone.'*

> *'We were told about various books – all of which I bought but weren't as much help as the other mums I met along my journey who are the only people who truly understand the situation.'*

It's a weird world you enter into when your child/partner is diagnosed with an ED and the quicker you accept this and take a step back from it the stronger you will be. You will become hyper aware of the slightest thing that someone may say or do that could be a trigger towards a downturn in your child's well-being.

You have to stop trying to fix it, you cannot save your child but you can support them, be there for them. I found this the hardest thing to acknowledge. As a parent you want to soothe your child's pain, it is so distressing not to be able to do that. You cannot make your child want to get better they have to want this for themselves. It is their responsibility. I consider this easier to accept when your child is over eighteen but I admire the incredible courage and wherewithal of parents who do this when their child is twelve, thirteen or even younger.

> '...I came to the point of knowing that I couldn't make a difference. Early on when I used the B-eat website a lot I was told by an anorexic: "Mummy, sticking plasters can't fix this." That hurt but in retrospect was the honest truth.'

Counselling and Therapy

There were lasting effects that I wasn't aware of for a long time after my daughter was well on the path to recovery. It hadn't even crossed my mind to think that I would be affected by all this, once it was over surely it was over? When my daughter was well on the road to recovery and I didn't need to be on a constant state of alert, I consequently found myself extremely tired and weepy for, as I thought, no reason at all.

> 'The most help I had was three years of behavioural therapy with an amazingly experienced therapist, who let me just rant when I needed to... that was a time when I could focus. No one knows how you feel, you can lose your identity to anorexia as well... as everyone cares and asks about the sufferer.'

If I had to face this a second time around I would definitely make sure I took better care of myself. It's tough and demanding on both body and soul. Don't neglect yourself. If you wear yourself out and get stressed and ill, who will take care of your child? It's important to keep yourself well. It's also setting an example to your child that you are worthy of love and care and so, as a consequence, are they. You may end up needing counselling and support. I did, afterwards and six years later, writing this book has made me realise how I am still affected by this time of my life. Two sets of counselling later and I was sitting at my desk, researching and writing, and all the anxious feelings came back, my heart racing, stomach churning and it didn't calm down for days. It took me by surprise, I had thought I was past all that and then I was angry, in fact downright furious. I hated that damn condition so much and the power it had over me, I wanted to kill that damn Bitch voice that steals our beautiful children away.

> *'Get as much support as possible. Find as much info as you can. Look after yourself too. Get others involved (family/husband). Husbands usually get pushed aside feeling left out, unhelpful.'*

I watched a news item on breakfast TV about a girl who had written a book about her eating disorder. She said her father had read through it but not her mother, it still upset her so much. I knew exactly how that mother felt and when they showed a photo of the girl when she weighed so very little I burst into tears. The shock and horror of it all. Nelly was never that thin and my heart broke for the parents who daily watch their children suffer in this way. Why, oh why, are we bringing our children into a world where they feel they are ugly and unworthy? And figures rise all the time – girls as well as boys.

> *'…it has put a massive amount of stress on the family. We all feel that we have lost our daughter/sister, etc. she has been completely taken over by the ED. It was difficult to juggle hospital visits and appointments with working full time and also trying to support my other daughter who was going through her GCSEs at the time. Since discharge the ED has consumed all of our lives. My daughter is on strictly reduced activities so cannot go out*

*and do much, she will also only eat at home
and not in front of anyone else – so family life
has become so isolated. Cannot go to friends
for food, nor can we invite them to ours,
cannot have lunch or dinner out anywhere.'*

Talking through my problems with a therapist showed
me how I was blocking out the bad things to get
through each challenge I met in life, and how I
gradually came to a brick wall that I couldn't get over,
under or around. I will always be grateful that my
doctor spotted the signs of depression and referred me
to therapy. It has made my life so much better and I
have energy that I thought I would never have again.

It may not be for you but don't dismiss it out of hand
– and please don't feel you have failed if you do so. The
struggle you are going through is absolutely punishing.
Be kind to yourself.

Support Groups
Support is crucial. EDs are so isolating – who can you
freely talk to who won't judge you or freak out when
you tell them about some of the behaviour your child
or partner may exhibit? It's a relief to talk to someone
whose face doesn't pale, whose eyebrows don't rise,
whose lips don't form a thin line as they bite back
words not to leap in with well intentioned advice. We
laugh, we cry, we root for each other and our collective
children to get well. I'm energised when I leave,
acknowledged, understood, normal. Our children are
all ages, some under eighteen, many over. There are
those who slip over the line to adulthood whilst their
parents attend the group and that's when the support
ends for the child and changes into adult care and you

have to start all over again.

> *'Go to family therapy. It's daunting but it's*
> *great to meet other parents and realise you are*
> *not the only one.'*

Many are run by the clinics where your child may be receiving treatment. I didn't attend these whilst Nelly was receiving treatment as they clashed with my work. I started going when I was writing this and found enormous support and help. I can't tell you how good it feels to sit and cry and rant and feel like you aren't going mad – and to hear other parents say they feel the same as you. It was so good to be in a room where I didn't have to make excuses or try and turn the conversation to something less stressful.

Many are informal, a place to sit and chat about how good or bad your week has been, to celebrate progress however small that might be. They are a valuable resource of information and support. Some parents have been through the experience and come out the other side. While it may be quite frightening from some perspectives to hear just how bad things can get, there will ultimately be someone who has already been in the situation you are now facing. They will be able to offer you hope and a shoulder to cry on but also practical help – about finances, care and many other things you may not even have thought of.

> *'Work colleagues/friends were so supportive,*
> *as were my mum and cousin. Family therapy*
> *was useful too, although if I'm honest, we*
> *didn't ever want to go. Met some lovely people*
> *though.'*

They may be held at the clinic/hospital where your child is receiving help, or may be run by a small independent charity set up by ex-sufferers or parents. I've attended both and gained something different from each one. The clinic based groups have a member of the medical staff from the centre on hand and sometimes introduce a specialist speaker on things as diverse as body image, different therapy forms, and where to get financial advice and support, and so on. Some units will have books you can borrow and there is always a qualified practitioner available so that you can ask questions or get pertinent advice for your situation which I found really important.

However, as with any group, I would caution to go only when it gives you support and uplifts you, so that you leave feeling stronger than you did when you arrived. It's so easy to get dragged down worrying about things you've heard and that won't help you at all.

'I told everyone. I didn't want anyone to go through the same as us, and I wasn't ashamed of what had happened to our daughter. It transpired that a few of my friends had had anorexia themselves as youngsters and they were great listeners. My husband and I also joined our local carers group with like-minded parents and although it didn't give us any answers, it was nice to know we weren't going through this on our own. After we moved house…we joined the carers group there too.'

Chapter 21: Friends, Family and Carers

What a minefield this can be. Most people I've encountered that don't have first-hand experience of an eating disorder think that telling the person to eat more, fatten themselves up, have a good roast dinner, etc., is the solution to everything. If you can talk to them do so – if not, best to avoid them in a small group setting. It can be like sitting in a pot of water and waiting for it to boil. Although having had hot flushes – or power surges as my friend likes to call them – the feeling is on a parallel. An extremely uncomfortable place to be.

> *'My colleagues were amazingly supportive. My cousin has experience in this area – also brilliant. Most other people were on a need-to-know basis. Generally, people don't understand.'*

Friends are so important; you need to find normality in all the turmoil but you need to be selective. I quickly learned that when a friend asked how things were going I had to tailor my response to suit. Don't stay around people who make you feel bad, it feels dire enough without having some condescending person you thought was a friend make you feel that she knows damn well, that if she were in your place, she would do things much differently, and huh, as if she'd let her child get into that state anyway. The negativity will drain you of your energy and resources and they are far too valuable to throw away on people that don't matter.

*'I have confided in it to a number of close
friends taking the view that it was better
discussed and out in the open. This approach
has helped me deal with the emotional issues
that have arisen with the eating disorder and
given me strength to cope with helping my
daughter.'*

Family can be even more tricky – it's harder to ignore
them. The immediate family will be coping in whatever
way they can.

*'We shut ourselves away as a family. They
were too shocked and even to this day,
grandparents, aunts and uncles do not
understand why she could not just eat. Today
she looks well but no one can understand that
she still has major issues going on inside her
head.'*

Family gatherings, occasions such as Christmas, Easter,
birthdays and anniversary celebrations can loom like a
monster in the distance. If you can avoid them do so, if
not then have a strategy. Keep your ears open and try
to diffuse potential explosive points of contact. If your
child wants to sulk, let them (sometimes), and keep
well-meaning relatives at bay. I became an expert at
circumventing conversations and whilst I am quite sure
on some occasions I must have sounded quite mad, I
really didn't care. I would rather they thought I was
losing the plot than they trigger a situation that I would
have to cope with on my own when I got back home.

'*Extended family and friends were told over the next couple of weeks when I was a bit surer of what was happening. There were some friends and family members that I didn't tell because of the taboo around EDs – I felt embarrassed/guilty perhaps? I explained it as the sickness syndrome that they already knew she had anyway. Most people that I did tell were shocked and disbelieving but also supportive. Though the level of ignorance around the understanding of EDs was astounding. A few comments like "well, she has to stop being a faddy eater now" and "if it was my child I would just make her eat" were really unhelpful and totally ignorant.*'

Sometimes, although well meaning, those you love, dear family and friends just don't understand. I wouldn't have understood if I'd have been on the outside looking in on my friend. I would only have seen the pain and anguish my sister/friend was going through and wondered why she couldn't just get a grip. If only it were that easy.

A word of advice to friends and family
Don't judge. Walk a mile in their shoes – and you'll have stolen someone else's shoes. Yes, it's really important to keep a sense of humour and that's what friends are for. Go out, to the theatre, the movies, go swimming, take afternoon tea. Do something restorative at least once a day. Try and maintain a little pocket of normality in your life. It will help so much.

'My daughter and her younger sister were constantly battling and I can understand why now I think my eldest daughter compared herself with her younger sibling and was envious that she didn't care what and how much she ate. My eldest daughter wanted her sister to eat as much as she needed to when getting well. It led to constant arguments and tears. My husband and I had our moments when we argued, but in general we were there for each other.'

'Our family were brilliant, now that I look back. We did all pull together, but it was a really horrible time. We tried to give lots of support to our youngest daughter without our eldest knowing, as we didn't want her to feel guilty.'

Helplines

If you can't get to a group but really need to talk to someone try calling one of the helplines mentioned in the resources section of this book. You will find someone who can be there to simply listen but also be available for advice and direction when you are at the end of your tether.

80 per cent never go to the doctors at all; 95 per cent contact via email or website (www.b-eat.co.uk)

Carers

As you may have experienced, it's mainly mum, and sometimes dad, but without a doubt, no one in the home situation is unaffected when someone suffers

133

with an eating disorder in the family.

*'Me and my other daughter have been
supporting each other. My ex partner is OK
but we have problems from time to time. Some
good friends have been really supportive.'*

It's helpful if you can talk about it and form a united
front. You will have to be flexible as each day will bring
something different and you won't quite know what
you will have to deal with. If there are other children in
the family situation, especially teenagers with
hormones all over the place – the stress can be palpable.

*'My husband kept everything around us
going.'*

As with all things, I've learned that talking about
problems and worries instead of keeping them held in
can do a lot to turn a fraught situation into something
more manageable. Keep all lines of communication
open whenever you can.

Chapter 22: Consequences of an Eating Disorder

Many people make the assumption that the only consequence of an eating disorder is loss of weight. If only that were the sum of it. The repercussions are far wider and deeper than what sits on the surface. Here are some of them:

Your child

- Debt through not turning up at work due to illness. Overspending on clothes but more commonly food to binge then purge – this can cost a terrific amount.
- Losing friends, becoming withdrawn and secretive, isolating themselves to avoid criticism or being 'found out'.
- Avoiding family gatherings, meals out, and special occasions because they feel everyone will be looking at them with loathing.
- Education – may drop out of university or college because they are too tired to concentrate or get panic attacks.
- Health – strain on their internal organs. Dental decay from vomiting. Poor nutrition, weakened immune system.
- Fertility – periods can stop and they may take a long time to be restored to any regular pattern.

Many of those with eating disorders get into debt. Most often they can't work because they are so weak from lack of food, or they can't concentrate. As a parent carer you can lose pay or your job because you are looking after them, taking them to appointments, etc. or you just can't keep your mind on the job any more. A survey carried out in 2015 by PricewaterhouseCoopers for B-eat, the UK eating disorders charity, estimates that £15 billion per annum is the cost of eating disorders.

Chapter 23: Constructive Steps to Help Your Child Recover

How I wish I had one perfect answer for you here – a one size fits all method that was proven to work whatever your situation. Until I find one, or you do (please let me know) here are some things that might help you cope through the days and weeks ahead.

Dos and Don'ts

Do separate the behaviour from your child
When your child is in the grip of an eating disorder it's so easy to fall into the trap of criticising them because they can't (or you feel they won't) do the one simple thing that will stop you worrying. Don't play the blame game. Your child is not the eating disorder. Avoid placing shame, blame or guilt on the person and their behaviours.

'Rudeness is not a symptom of anorexia.'
Eating Disorders: Helping your child recover:
Steve Bloomfield

Do have boundaries
Set aside some quiet time to think about what you will and will not put up with. Talk it over with your partner if you have one, a good friend or someone who will make you feel supported and give you clarity. For example, one of my boundaries was that we would all sit and eat at the table as normal. If Nelly didn't want to join us, fine, but we, as a family, did not have an eating disorder and we would not change our eating habits.

Do discuss things with your partner
This is especially important if you are divorced or separated. It's easy for them to say they have eaten at the other parent's home and play one against the other. The eating disorder will thrive in an environment of secrets. You need to pull together on this if nothing else for the sake of your child – and your sanity.

Do tell them you are concerned
It's important that they know you care and want them to be well even if they don't want it for themselves. Repeat as necessary.

Do avoid simple solutions
There is no quick fix answer. One meal will not mean they are on the road to recovery. It will take time, more time than you can imagine and then some. You have to realise that you are in this for the long haul, there will be good days and many, many bad days but consistency and celebrating small successes goes a long way to keeping steady on the road to recovery.

Do develop distractions for mealtimes
Sit with them until they have finished their food and it has time to be digested. Watch a movie, read, play board games, talk, play I Spy – anything to distract until the urge to purge passes or subsides.

> *'Best strategies: DISTRACTION! – we were taught this many times at family therapy. That and colouring. Loombands were the favourite distraction. We will never play with them now!'*

138

Do develop distractions for after mealtimes

Don't let them go to the bathroom immediately after finishing a meal. They are going there to be sick. Stay with them, distract them, and if they do go to the loo go with them. Yes, I know, mortifying isn't it? I didn't ever go in the cubicle, I stood outside and made her talk to me (constantly) or we would sing along together – she couldn't sing and be sick so that kept her on track. And I have no shame. I made her sing in service stations and restaurants, cafes and bars. I would not let her get away with it once I knew. Get a handy repertoire and, if all else fails, the alphabet or times table will do.

Do get support – good support

Yes, I know I've talked about it before but it's so important that I am saying it again here. Join a care group if you can find one, preferably a specific group for those who are caring for sufferers of eating disorders. Join one online and you can rant and rave with people who get it any time of the day or night. Online groups are usually populated by parents from all over the world and they are generous in sharing strategies, up-to-date treatment and things that they have found useful.

Do ask for help

Most important of all. You can't do this alone, well, of course you can but please don't. I wish I'd asked for help earlier rather than soldiering on thinking I should have all the answers simply because I was her mother. Blaming myself stopped me from asking for help when I could have done with some objective support and advice. It might have provided damage limitation for my own mental health if not for hers.

> '(I) went into a world of my own, totally cut
> out everyone – tried to find out as much info
> as I could from books/internet. Didn't know
> how or what to tell anyone and didn't think
> they would understand and I felt stupid like it
> was my fault. Why didn't I see it? Where was
> I, how could I not know? What was going on?
> Why couldn't she tell me? So many emotions.
> I just put up a barrier and committed myself
> to fighting ED.'

Do take time for yourself
See the section on self-care. If you only get to read a
book, watch your favourite TV show, go dancing. Do it.
Anything that gives you respite is worth its weight in
gold.

Do trust your gut feeling
If you think something's wrong it usually is. Trust that
instinct and follow it through until you are satisfied.

> 'Don't be fooled, be honest with yourself and
> them all the time, keep lines of communication
> open as much as you can. Don't ever forget
> that this has the highest mortality rate of any
> mental health illness.'

Do keep asking questions
Ask your child, your doctor, the clinic; be a pain in the
derrière if needs must, but make sure you are informed
every step of the way.

'SHOUT!! Don't be afraid to get the help you need for your child. Make yourself heard and make a nuisance of yourself so that people don't forget you. Attend every workshop, meeting, counselling session that you can. Look after yourself first so that you can look after your child. And just remember that the responsibility is that of the sufferer and they won't get better for anyone else but themselves, so if they are in denial about being ill, there is nothing on God's earth you can do to help them get better. You just have to support them, and make sure that they are safe.'

Do talk to other people
Talk to your partner, talk to your children. Everyone is feeling crap about the situation. I know how angry my son was that I was so upset and worn out dealing with the problem. Did he resent his sister for putting me through this turmoil? Again, I never asked him and in retrospect I should have talked to him about it – but only if he had wanted to. Most likely I didn't open up that conversation because I was so tired from muddling along day after day. The same reason I didn't write about it or keep a diary. He's a parent now himself so will have a better understanding of the lengths you will go to to protect your child but it was still tough on him and I regret that.

Don't think if you ignore it, it will go away.
It won't.

Don't think it will get better by itself.
It won't.

Don't think that your child would never get an eating disorder
That's the mistake I made. I had totally discounted it as I thought my daughter was the last person on earth that would have problems with her food. Well, let me say it again in case you didn't get it the first time, IT'S NOT ABOUT THE FOOD!

Don't think it only happens to young, white, middle class girls
It can happen to anyone, boys, young men and women, older men and women although the facts are that it's highest among the under eighteens. However, how many people out there are managing without support and slipping under the mental health radar?

Don't assume it was something you did as a parent
Most likely it wasn't. There are many factors that come together to create an eating disorder. Blaming yourself will not help you; it will drain you and stop you from thinking objectively when you need to.

Don't make assumptions
I assumed that I wasn't allowed to talk to the doctors and they weren't allowed to talk to me. I could have asked for advice, I could have asked more questions, asked for help. I should have been more assertive. During research for this book I requested a meeting with Dr Ciarán Newell, Consultant Nurse at Kimmeridge Court, the specialist eating disorders clinic in Poole. I had never asked for a meeting with any of

the medical staff whilst my daughter was receiving treatment there. Part of me thought I would be shut out, she was over eighteen, another part of me was aware of the stresses on the NHS and I did not want to waste a scrap of their time talking to me when they could be helping someone who was ill. I felt such an idiot when Dr Newell, my own doctor, said he could have answered any questions I had about eating disorders without discussing my daughter's case. I blundered around because I was too polite and too passive. I am developing a directness as far as that is concerned and you would be as well to develop it too. Being polite can cost you time, precious time. You need to be informed.

'I don't regret any of the rows I have had with health professionals. I don't regret begging (her) to eat or trying to trick her into eating stuff. Of course, in an ideal world I would rather we hadn't gone on this journey and I have sat in many, many mental health facilities wondering what on earth I have done to deserve this, but we have survived and we are surviving and I am doing everything I can to support B-eat with fundraising, and making other people aware of this awful illness by talking to them and supporting them. I am not ashamed of what has happened and I will do anything in my power to ensure that other people don't suffer as we have.'

Don't isolate yourself

It's easy to hide away. Many people feel embarrassed, many are afraid of what people will say or think – you only have to tell one person and get a bad reaction and it makes you clam up. Choose wisely – join a support group either real or online. Friendly support can be reassuring and it's strengthening to be with people with who are going through or have been through exactly the same circumstances.

Don't be passive

If you're not getting the help you need make a noise. Look elsewhere, don't be fobbed off by bad treatment or non-existent treatment. Keep searching. Join support groups, get on Facebook and Twitter, ask questions, find out what other people did to get their child well, what worked and what didn't work for them. One little thing they say may be the route to getting good help and support in a place you never thought of looking.

> *'Read, read and read – take on as much knowledge as you can. Understanding the ED is crucial. Go to any training or support groups. Talk openly and honestly with the person who has the ED – even difficult conversations like discussing their suicidal thoughts is much better out in the open. And patience, you need a lot of patience – there is no magic wand – recovery is slow and painful, relapses always happen, but you have to keep going, you have to keep the hope going because the person with the ED may not have any hope or desire to get better.'*

Don't convey fat prejudice or reinforce the desire to be thin
Try not to show disappointment, there will be setbacks, you may take two steps forward and three back. Maintaining an equal demeanour is draining and you want to scream in frustration and despair but try your best. It will be best in the long run.

Don't think you're overreacting because they are teenagers
Challenge it.
Don't accept their manipulation of media to justify extreme exercise or odd eating patterns. Don't let them hide behind reports of the UK obesity crisis or anything they've heard or read that extols the virtues of the Paleo Diet, no-sugar diets and any other extreme life style choices they may have seen on Instagram. If you think something is wrong it usually is.

It pays to be blunt!
Don't skirt around the edges of things. You don't have time to be polite.

Chapter 24: Fear and Stress – The Killer Combination

Fear

The science bit: fear is an emotional response to danger, real or perceived. It is the perceived threat we need to conquer. My overriding fear was that my daughter would die – in fact ever since the day they were born perhaps my only fear was that I would lose my children. What I realised when I faced that fear instead of avoiding it may help you too. What if she had died? I felt at the time that I couldn't have borne the pain. But I would have. People have to bear that pain every day of their lives when they lose a child and that pain never, ever goes away, they just learn to live with it and carry on.

The thought of what might happen runs away with us and, the thing is, it's exhausting living with a child with an eating disorder, constantly anticipating their next move. It's tiring and wearing and this in turn breeds more fear and anxiety. You have to try and remove yourself from the vicious circle. Fear driven adrenaline is bad for us and I felt mine pumping twenty-four hours a day. No wonder I was both working manically and exhausted at the same time, there was no respite, no down time unless I was absolutely spent, then I was too tired to think of the consequences. One night I was in the house on my own and I heard a noise downstairs. Was it intruders? I lay in bed wondering whether to bother getting up and check what it was but the mere thought was too exhausting to contemplate. Instead of tensing up I thought well, just let them kill me, I'm too tired to move. It hardly seemed worth the effort to get off the bed let alone fight for my own life, I had been too busy fighting for my child's.

Fear exhausts and weakens you. It depletes your physical energy but also your immune system. Everything shifts out of balance. It creates that familiar churning in your stomach that will only be quietened by eating something comforting. For me, eating suppressed my anxiety, made me forget how scared I was. I ate to forget the pain and I worked to forget the pain. I see that I conquered this by filling my days with things. It didn't matter if they were meaningful, important or even productive. I was a boat tossed about on choppy waves, repeatedly baling out water to stay afloat. You have to counteract this before you sink – get some help. You may be able to swim, or even walk to the shore but you're so focused on sinking that you can't look around you and see where you really are. Get out of the damn boat! Even if it's only a day trip, for heaven's sake, give yourself a break.

Fear is instinct, we don't consciously trigger it. I could tell you all the scientific details about what part triggers the brain and so on but it wouldn't help. There are finer writers to tell you that and to tell the truth, understanding the science of your brain doesn't help when you are lying awake thinking of tactics and strategies that will help get your child back on the road to health. Understanding my brain and reactions – or hers – didn't help at all. There are children with parents who are scientists and psychologists who have depression and mental illness too. Just because you know how it works it doesn't mean that you can avoid the problems caused by difficult mental health. What you have to do is learn coping strategies – like singing in the toilet and going round the roundabout three times. You have to find the little tricks that lift you out of the spiral and up onto the surface again so that you can bob about and try and spot the shore.

Stress

Stress is not a bad thing, it keeps our minds sharp and keeps us alert but too much stress and we start to make ourselves ill, we overload our systems. Learning to cope with the overload is key.

Again, get some support. Many of us live away from extended family – and that can be good or bad – if you don't get on with your family it might be the best way of dealing with a stressful situation that you can't change. It's all down to perspective. But we don't live as we used to any more, keeping in touch face to face. My mother lives 300 miles away and I speak to her every day but when times were really tough I wouldn't tell her as I didn't want her to worry more than she already did. That said, she could tell by the sound of my voice if I was in a good place or not. Still, it's not the same as talking to her at the kitchen table, sharing a cup of tea.

As with fear, you need to develop a strategy that gives you respite so that you can build up your reserves. I've included things that might help in the section on self-care; but the main thing to remember is to develop your own escape route that will enable you to step out of the cycle of fear and stress – because there can be enough to deal with in the present.

'Seeing her in hospital with drips and oxygen when my daughter said she didn't want to live any more. Because she was useless, worthless and she told me I couldn't help her and she hated me.'

'Her first overdose at a weight of five stone and taking fifty-seven tablets of various strengths was a very risky thing to do and I would say that it was probably my lowest point. But over the last two years there have been many terrible moments, which I have survived and have made me stronger and more tolerant and a better person.
Also, the self-harming (cutting her arms and legs) makes me sad because that is a reminder forever as to what she has done.'

'This whole episode is one that I have to draw strength from and find a positive in it, otherwise I would go crazy myself.'

Chapter 25:   Consequences for You

You may find, as I experienced, that your life shrinks rapidly. You stop doing things because you don't have the energy and are worried about what might happen. You dip out of going to family gatherings or meeting with friends because you're afraid it will trigger something, running through potential scenarios in your head and calculating possible exit strategies. It all becomes too much to bother with so you turn down all invitations. It's safer that way.

Weight gain

I started being hungry all the time. Other mothers I interviewed also put on weight – either consciously or subconsciously. Many sufferers cook and feed others without partaking themselves (Nelly did this). They use bartering – I'll eat this if you eat that – which you know will add the pounds but you do it, you do anything to get them to eat.

Debt

One of the worst consequences that can threaten the stability of you and your family is financial hardship. You may need time off work, or you may have to give up work completely. There are trips to hospitals, consultants, perhaps private treatments. The costs soon start mounting and there is nothing so debilitating as worrying about money. My one stop shop for most monetary information and advice is *www.moneysavingexpert.com* – easy to navigate and easy to read. But there are other places of support in the resources that follow.

Self care

What's that I hear you cry? With apologies to our American cousins we Brits aren't very good at it on the whole, especially mums who feel guilty about spending on themselves instead of their children. It's a habit that develops when they are born and you hold them in your arms and I'm not sure that it ever ends completely.

Most women, if making a list, would put their children first, husband next, dog/cat, house and home, and themselves last. Well, girls, get yourself to the top of that list along with your kids and your husband – and who says the list has to be vertical? It should be a horizontal – everyone of equal importance.

So in the spirit of indulgence on a novice level I offer the following just in case you've got badly out of practice. Start with something small.

Chapter 26: Self Care for Beginners

My mantra – Keep it Simple. It's hard to remember to take time for yourself. You don't need a huge budget, in fact you don't need anything other than the willingness to set aside time for yourself. That in itself can be the hardest mountain you have to climb. You are important, your health and well-being is important. Remember that. Repeat as necessary.

Baths

Ah, still my greatest luxury. I can be in there for hours. Red hot with plenty of top-ups. All you need is some Neal's Yard bath oil and a large immersion heater. Depends on your budget really but try to get something that smells indulgent and makes you feel a little decadent. My mum always used to hide the bath oil she ordered from Avon and if I found it, would steal a drop or two. You had to be careful getting out the bath as it was lethal and then I would have to give the bath a good clean to remove all evidence of my theft – but it was worth it. Buy something really feminine so the boys don't pinch it.

Bring out those candles that you received for Christmas and haven't taken out of the box yet because they are too good or pretty to burn and make sure you light them. Have one flickering flame lit to soothe you or go for it and get a bag of tea lights and use them all in one go. Pour yourself a glass of wine or a cuppa with instruction for refills in half an hour. Choose some soft background music and if you fancy reading, a good escapist book or magazine, and simply step into heaven. I could quite happily spend the entire evening in the bath like this. Nothing can deter me, not even reports that hot water is bad for your skin and will prematurely age you. I need my bath!

Walks
I find that walking the dog lifts my spirits enormously and it could well do the same for you. So walk the dog, walk someone else's dog. Borrow one if you don't have one of your own, much cheaper and you'll get two friends for life – firstly, the dog and secondly, the owner who you will be helping out. Whatever the weather a walk in the fresh air gives you time to think and clears the lungs. Going back into the house feels entirely different after a walk and will give you some much needed time for reflection and escape. My dog, Harry, bounds along the heath full of joy and curiosity, and even though when we return from jumping in puddles he is fond of shaking himself clean in the utility room, I don't mind. It is soon remedied. I learned long ago to paint the walls in vinyl silk. I simply enjoy his unfettered happiness and a little rubs off on me. There is not a thought in his head and I am still trying to allow myself that freedom instead of worrying about things that might never happen. I think dogs can teach us a lot about mindfulness – I think they invented it.

Celebrate the Ordinary
Make yourself afternoon tea, a proper one. Don't grab a mug and a Kit Kat. Bring out the teapot, add a beautiful cup and saucer and get yourself a generous slice of cake. My indulgence was carrot cake. And while we are on the subject of cakes, if you find it therapeutic to

make them yourself, go ahead. But if you're pushed for time the supermarket or a local bakery will do just as well. Make it a treat, get a nice plate, sit and savour it.

Make some cucumber sandwiches, cut the crusts off, slice them into fingers or triangles, have fun preparing it. The emphasis is on pleasure from start to finish.

It's so easy to always be focused on others, especially when your child is or isn't eating. Food becomes both a weapon and a slave. I lost the pleasure of food for a long time, I couldn't enjoy a meal because I was always focused on what everyone else was eating, how they were acting and reacting. Even snacks were eaten without thinking, the quick hit of a chocolate bar to keep me going rather than face the stress of preparation. When I was on my own I tried to eat properly, cooking from scratch, trying to set a good example but I didn't taste anything. It was food that had to be eaten. If this is happening to you try and break the pattern and give yourself space to enjoy the pleasure of food again.

> 'Tried...to catch up with friends, go for a walk, etc. not always easy to manage but it is important to take some time out for yourself. Wine – wine always helps!'

Pamper Days
Get your hair and nails done, take pride in yourself; it's so easy to blame yourself for what is happening. This leads to low self-esteem and self-worth and it's not a good example to set any of our children. Show your child you are worthy of love, worthy of a good life, as are we all. If you can't afford a salon find someone that you can barter with but please, please don't neglect

154

yourself. Get a friend to do your manicure in exchange for you walking their dog – see how I did that? Dogs can solve so many problems!

However, only do this if it makes you feel good. Conversely, if you have been putting on a 'face' to greet the world and conforming to the stereotype of having to have perfect nails, hair and clothes at all times then give yourself some time out. You may find that it's a wonderful release not to have to conform. The most important message here is to be yourself and be comfortable with who you are.

Eating Out
Go for a meal. Eat it and enjoy it without any pressure – even if it's a bag of chips sitting on a bench. Savour and enjoy every mouthful. I can't remember enjoying food at all when my daughter was ill even though I ate plenty of it. The best thing about going out for a meal was that I didn't have to clear up afterwards. I was too knackered by then.

Go out and have a meal, a relaxed meal, where you're not afraid of ordering what you want and eating it.

Plan an escape from the tension and keep food enjoyable. I would always take my mobile phone with me and leave it on the table, on silent, in case she needed me. I'm not sure that was a good thing but at the time I needed to know that if she needed me I would be there for her. Now, I wouldn't do that at all, I would get someone else on standby, give them my phone if need be. I would allow myself time out. Time and space to be in a restaurant without watching what she ate and then going off to the toilet with her so that she wasn't sick.

If you are worried about leaving your child alone, no matter how old they are, get a babysitter. It could be a friend, a grandparent, their boyfriend but you need to get out. You have to keep living your life.

Mindfulness

There's a lot to be said for living in the moment. You need to appreciate the small glories in life for there are many for each of us every day. How lucky we are to live in a country with beautiful scenery – whether that be of nature or architecture. We have hot and cold running water, we have fresh air to breathe, we live in peace not war. Yet inner war can be so damaging, as can worrying about things that might never happen. I used to be an absolute expert at that.

I've read many books about 'living in the moment' and although I could grasp what was meant it was so much harder to put in to practice. I don't want to give you reams of instruction here, or a list of recommended reading. I don't think that would be helpful.

I was always looking for something quick and easy, something that I could fit into my everyday life, no matter what was happening – and guess what? Mindfulness fits the bill perfectly.

Switch off your phone, the TV, the radio, put down your newspaper or tablet, and give yourself ten minutes of peace and stillness. Don't leave everything running in the background; it's not only distracting but it also makes our minds keep tuning in and out of what's going on around us, the world's interference. Sit in the bathroom if need be, lock the door.

Make yourself comfortable – lie down or simply

relax in a chair, put your hands on your lap, relax your shoulders. Now inhale deeply feeling your stomach expand, hold for a few seconds, then let out all of that stale breath as you slowly exhale. Repeat and feel yourself slowly relax into your breathing. If thoughts come into your mind try to let them slowly drift away with your breath. It may help to imagine yourself somewhere you feel really happy, like on a walk through woodland or green fields, lying on a beach, or observing a beautiful flower. It's akin to those times as a child when you would lie on your back in a field and watch the clouds scud by, totally absorbed and relaxed in the beauty of those pure white clouds in a gentle blue sky. After ten minutes of this quiet time you will feel yourself calmer and hopefully more able to cope with the day to day. Use it whenever you find a spare ten minutes. No, dammit, MAKE TEN MINUTES. You are worth it!

Stress reduction and relaxation
Be Mindful *www.bemindful.co.uk*
Mindful *www.mindful.org*

There is lots of useful and simple advice on being mindful to be found on both of these sites.

Cognitive Behavioural Therapy (CBT)
Your child may be receiving Cognitive Behavioural Therapy as part of their treatment but it can also help carers deal with the anxiety and stress that accompanies caring for someone with an eating disorder. A knowledgeable practitioner will guide you through your thought processes. It can't solve your

problems but it can help you think about them in a different way. We can get into a spiral of negative thinking which keeps us stuck, thinking that nothing is ever going to get better. CBT teaches you to stop the negative thoughts and helps you work in a practical way towards a more positive outlook on your situation. *www.nhs.uk/Conditions/Cognitive-behavioural-therapy*

Mental Health Foundation

Take the free stress test. You don't have to register and it's simply ten multiple choice questions.

There is a programme of ten easy to follow sessions with videos and interactive exercises.

12 assignments to practise day to day
5 guided meditation audio downloads
Online tools

Headspace

Try the mobile app for meditation made simple and sign up to Take Ten – a free ten day programme to learn the basics in ten minutes a day.
Find out more at *www.headspace.com*

Massage

Give it a try. It will relax you and soothe the stress and tension you hold in your body from trying to get through each day. I found myself hunched over the steering wheel as I drove, and slumped in a chair at the end of a day – massage helped enormously. Many local training colleges offer discounted sessions and treatments

EFT – Emotional Freedom Technique
EFT or Tapping as it is commonly called is easy to learn and easy to carry out. Pop over to YouTube and you'll find a variety of videos that you can follow. EFT is used as a healing tool with the focus on emotional issues as opposed to physical pain. It involves tapping with the fingertips at specific places on the body to stimulate the meridian points. Rooted in the Chinese meridian system it's akin to acupuncture and acupressure. *www.emofree.com*

Reiki
A healing therapy where the patient lays fully clothed on a therapy bed or couch. The therapist channels energy into the patient's body to activate the natural healing process. Balancing the chakras. Even if you don't believe, you will still find it soothing and relaxing and that is of benefit in itself. *www.reiki.org*

Yoga
'The practice of yoga helps to co-ordinate the breath, mind and body to encourage balance, both internally and externally and promote feelings of relaxation and ease.'
www.bwy.org.uk

A series of movements to promote strength and flexibility that can be a tremendous boost to your well-being. There are various types of yoga practice, from fast, hot, sticky, sweaty yoga to gentle stretches – you can even do yoga sitting down. There are plenty of classes in community centres and village halls as well as sports centres and specific yoga studios.

British Wheel of Yoga *www.bwy.org.uk* to find a class near you.

Enrol on a course

Many colleges and community centres offer evening and weekend classes on a variety of subjects. I've been absolutely shattered but when I went to a flower arranging class or yoga I would switch off and feel refreshed and re-energised afterwards. It's the action of getting out of your routine, being with other people that you probably only meet in that setting, that possibly know nothing about you and don't want to. They are there for the passion of learning, enjoyment, and that sense of escape. Distraction is so important. I once signed up for a class to make a Christmas wreath, racing to get there for 6.30pm, sitting in the car and taking a deep breath before I went in, feeling quite neurotic and frantic – and stupid that once again, I had tried to cram too much into the day. Yet, within minutes I had totally forgotten all my stresses of earlier and was happily sticking pine cones and polished conkers among the foliage. Walking out with my completed wreath I felt a sense of satisfaction, of accomplishment, there was actually something I could start and finish. Little successes are important and you can build on them.

> *'I knit. When I am stressed I knit squares and am making my "recovery blanket". I go to the gym and run, box, swim or do classes to take my mind off the awfulness of it all. I clean my house – for some reason it helps my stress and I have a VERY clean house now! No one told me these strategies. It's what I do.'*

Energetic stuff

While I prefer to walk the dog, do yoga, and participate in quieter pastimes I am beginning to wonder if I should have taken tae kwon do classes, Zumba, line dancing – something more exuberant. I've never been sporty or athletic, I've favoured quieter pursuits but I may have gained more if I'd stepped out of my comfort zone and tried something totally opposite to what I enjoyed. It might have exorcised a lot of the anger I held in my body, it might have released the aggression that I turned towards myself. Many massages and treatments later I feel less aches and pains and wonder if I could have avoided them altogether by being more vigorously active. The only way I can let my anger out is on the page, which I do quite frequently now, writing how angry this whole damn shit has made me but at least I know I can destroy the pages afterwards. And there is a gentle satisfaction in letting it burn and die.

I'd recommend you try anything, absolutely anything to make life more bearable and also to mix with people where you don't have to talk about all the crap that's going on at home.

Go for it. Enjoy yourself – it's infectious. Show your child how to live life every day.

If you're looking for something more vigorous why not try any of the following:

Climbing   Abseiling   Quad Biking   Roller Skating
Kick Boxing   Boogie Bounce   Zumba   Martial Arts

Movie Therapy: Films to make you laugh and cry

Watch old movies, a weepy, have a good cry, it will make you feel better and let out some of those pent up emotions that are depleting you. It gives you a chance to escape somewhere else for a while. Then after you've emptied yourself of tears hunt those comedies down. A good belly laugh is food for the soul and makes you forget your worries for a while. Laughter truly is the best medicine. If you can't find a movie you like, watch a DVD of your favourite comedian who'll make you laugh at the absurdity of life.

Check out *www.cinematherapy.com*

Here you will find a listing of films that will make you laugh, make you cry, make you feel good to be alive. The films are categorised according to emotional well-being, films for eating disorders, anxiety, grief and so on.
You can also read: *Movie Therapy: How it Changes Lives* by Bernie Wooder

Reading Therapy (bibliotherapy): Books for well-being

I'm an avid reader but when I was stressed I found that I couldn't read long fiction because I couldn't hold the story in my head. I became tired of flicking back through the pages because I couldn't remember who the characters were and what had happened in earlier chapters. But if you are looking for a book to suit your mood then check out the online resource *www.booksastherapy.com*
 You may also want to take a look at the books offered on the *Reading Well* programme established by *The Reading Agency*. This has two strands *Reading Well: Books on Prescription Scheme* and *Reading Well: Mood Boosting Books*.

Working with libraries, the scheme has been developed in partnership with the Society of Chief Librarians with funding from Arts Council England. Books on Prescription helps you manage and understand your health and well-being using self-help reading. The books have been recommended by experts.

Mood Boosting Books, recommended by readers, promote uplifting novels, non-fiction and poetry.

Learn more at *www.readingagency.org.uk*

Music Therapy: Music to soothe and inspire
Try Spotify on your computer or phone; playlists to suit your mood that you can switch on and let the music wash over you.

Go through all those old CDs that are filling the shelves. Some of them you won't have listened to for months, perhaps years. Get something upbeat and dance around the room, Pharrell Williams' 'Happy' is a great mood changer.

You can't fail but feel happy. For a time anyway, and even if you don't, what's wrong with faking it till you make it? You will feel happy again but until that time you need every bit of help you can grasp at to get there.

Art therapy
Absorb yourself with creating something of beauty, though I'm not sure anything I create could be called beautiful. A wobbly pot and a lopsided pig were about my limit at school and I haven't touched a lump of clay since, but playing around with it now would be fun. It's not the end result that counts it's the process we're

talking about here. The target is to relax and unwind and take your mind off your troubles. If you get a fruit bowl out of it, well done to you.

I've recently found an art class that suits me perfectly. The tutor is amazing and totally 'gets' me and what I want to get out of the lessons. It's not about creating something simple to sell but simply creating. There is no 'purpose' to my three hours in her studio merely 'play'. This lack of 'purpose' is such great fun that it totally invigorates me and makes me playful in all other aspects of my life.

Zentangle and adult colouring books

Zentangle is drawing images by creating structured patterns. It improves focus and creativity but I include it here just as another method to switch off from your everyday cares. It's relaxing as well as fun and almost creates a state of meditation.

As are the explosion in the Adult Colouring Books if you are stressed and anxious. It makes you calm down almost instantly and trying to keep within the lines is settling and soothing. Watching the colour grow is pleasing to the eye. If mindfulness is all about staying in the moment and you have difficulty with that then these books are a great alternative.

Hands off, kids and grandkids, these are MY crayons and it's MY book.

Gardening

Better than a gym and I used to think cheaper until I became addicted to garden centres. Still, there's nothing like tending your garden and watching things grow to restore your faith in the world. Even after the harshest of winters the snowdrops and daffodils still emerge to greet the sun and that's what will happen to you eventually. The sun will come back into your life no matter how tough things get.

> *'They will be that person again when they recover.'*

Self-care is about looking after yourself but as I read back the examples I've given I think it's more about an escape, going to a place within yourself where you are not constantly churning over your troubles and worrying yourself to distraction. Find some that work for you and keep them in your self-care armoury. When the going gets tough, as it will, the tough get their pens out and get colouring.

You will be engaging your brain and concentrating with the task in hand. This concentration gives the part of your brain that is doing the worrying a break. Relief! While you are trying to sculpt that bit of clay into something that isn't embarrassing you'll have moments when you realise that hours have gone by and all you've thought about was creating a bowl that wasn't wonky.

And lastly, look forward to happier times, they will come. Having a sense of humour does help, it gets you through the darker moments.

> *'She has kept her wonderful sense of humour through most of the past two years. When admitted...we all went up to the hospital...and she was taken off by the nurses to have some lunch whilst we were spoken to by other care professionals. When (she)*

*returned she said to me that she thought she
was going to starve in there as the portions
were so small!! A small chink of light in a
very bleak day.'*

*'Being shown the pile of Ensure bottles
dropped out of the toilet window when she
was supposed to be on one-to-one nursing.
Being able to take being sworn at and called
all vile names may reduce you to tears but
afterwards can actually be quite amusing that
there is so much fire.'*

For a simple ten step guide to stress busting use the
following link

*http://psychcentral.com/blog/archives/2009/03/18/10-stress-
busters/*

Resources

There are many places to get help and support and resources are growing all the time as sadly, eating disorders and other mental health problems continue to increase. Or perhaps there has always been a huge problem but people are now more able to talk about it? Whatever your opinion on this the results are the same – you need to find help, and find it fast.

These are some of the available places of support in the UK and if they can't help you in the first instance they will be able to direct you to the appropriate route to support and advice. I have limited these resources as I could go on and on and that would only confuse. Starting with any one of these institutions will lead you towards the help or support you seek.

Practical Support

B-eat – The UK's Eating Disorder Charity

Helpline 0845 634 1414
www.b-eat.co.uk

The B-eat Adult Helpline is open to anyone over eighteen who needs support and information relating to an eating disorder, including sufferers, carers and professionals.

Helplines are open on Monday and Wednesday from 12 noon to 8.30pm and Tuesday, Thursday and Friday from 12 noon to 5pm.

The website is a first stop for many who discover their child or partner has an eating disorder. There are a variety of resources online and as with any web based resource it is changing and developing all the time as new research and support methods become available.

Emotional Support

Samaritans

Helpline 08457 90 90 90
www.samaritans.org

Available 24 hours a day 365 days a year.

Talking can really help you get perspective and the relief of getting things out will leave you feeling unburdened. They won't interrupt, give you advice or tell you what to do but will listen and quite often basic things, like listening, are the most precious. You don't have to be suicidal to use the help they offer. If life is getting you down and you don't know where to turn try giving them a call.

I particularly liked this quotation from their website "They are there when all your friends are asleep and you are alone in the world, full of thoughts". Being alone with our thoughts is quite often the loneliest and scariest time. Please don't be afraid to call thinking that your problem is too small.

Advice and support on mental health issues

Mind

Helpline 0300 123 3393
www.mind.org.uk

A great one stop shop for help and advice – how to help someone with a mental health problem, how to get help for yourself, financial and legal advice, down to earth practical advice.

The website is easy to access and navigate and won't bog you down with too much information.

Young Minds

Parent helpline 0808 802 5544
www.youngminds.org.uk

Various resources to give support for young people up to the age of twenty-five with mental health problems.

They provide a free and confidential service and the parent helpline is a great place to start if you need someone to talk to and guidance on where to get further help.

There is a section for parents worried about their children. It will direct you to the information relating to eating disorders.

Rethink

Helpline 0121 522 7007
www.rethink.org

Rethink Mental Illness. Comprehensive sections on how and where to get support for yourself and for your child. You will find information on how to support someone with suicidal thoughts, how to respond to the behaviour of someone with a mental health problem. Free factsheets, help and advice on work, finances and debt with localised helplines around the country. They also offer lots of support for siblings.

The website has a superb, downloadable free booklet that I would encourage you to read. It won't take you too long, it's not too exacting but simply explains what stress is, how it affects you mentally and physically and encourages you in a clear and practical way how to set up a support process for yourself when times get tough.

http://www.rethink.org/media/528995/CFY_8_Taking_Care_of_Yourself.pdf

National Centre for Eating Disorders

Helpline 0845 838 2040
www.eating-disorders.org.uk

Useful information for carers.
www.eating-disorders.org.uk/information/your-loved-one-has-an-ed/

Health Talk

www.healthtalk.org

Health talk provides free, reliable information about health issues by sharing people's real-life experiences.

www.healthtalk.org/young-peoples-experiences/eating-disorders/myths-about-eating-disorders

Other Regional Resources

SWEDA – Somerset and Wessex Eating Disorders Association

01749 671318
www.swedauk.org

Restored Bournemouth

07959 378822
www.restoredcharity.wordpress.com

First Steps, Derbyshire

01332 367571
www.firststepsderbyshire.co.uk

Life Works

08081497476
www.lifeworkscommunity.com

Social Media as a Resource

Facebook Pages
If you can't find a support group near you then try the internet support groups. If you simply want to rant at the unfairness and ugliness of the situation then go ahead. It's allowed! The wonderful thing about these closed groups is that they provide a safe place to get information and to let off steam. No one is going to judge you, they know exactly where you are coming from, and knowing that is a gift in itself.

Facebook Groups
I've listed three below but I am sure there are others. Again, I am keeping things simple and offer these as a starting point.

- FEAST
- Around the Dinner Table
- Peer Support for Parents of Children with Eating Disorders

You have to ask to join and be accepted. You will swiftly be deleted if you are a rogue member and looking to sell something or promote your business. These groups are run by parents for parents. Although there are many parents wanting to rant and cry with rage against this illness, the system, the medical profession, etc., there are also many people whose children are in recovery and the hope they can give is amazing. Just what you need when you feel no one understands. And it's there 24/7 for those nights when you just can't sleep.

Twitter accounts

All major charities around the world have Twitter accounts and you can access links to up-to-date research and resources. By the time this book is published much of it may be out of date but social media is a quick and easy way of getting the latest information. However, as there is so much information available out there you can tire yourself keeping track. I would advise you to look at a selection and settle with one or two that appeal and stick with them. It can be gruelling trying to keep on top of everything and you end up no wiser and with your energy depleted to boot. You can also scare yourself silly as I did when carrying out Google searches.

Sometimes it's akin to wandering down many paths, getting lost in a maze of information. I honestly found more support and comfort from listening to other parents/carers and sharing what worked and what didn't on a personal basis but you have to discover what works best for you – and not everyone has great internet access or even the accessibility of transport to attend groups that may exist locally.

> *'Living offshore made everything harder to access. You can't attend a carer's meeting due to distance and cost.'*

Financial support

Where to get help and what you can expect to get help with: government help as well as available grants can be found on the websites mentioned above.

According to a report commissioned by B-eat from PricewaterhouseCoopers, the impact of eating disorders costs £15 billion per annum.

This can be in lost time at work, taking time off to attend appointments or losing your job altogether. It could be because you either get sacked or because you can no longer juggle all the balls in the air.

You can read the full report by using the link below:
http://www.b-eat.co.uk/research/summary-of-completed-research/913-pwc-2015-the-costs-of-eating-disorders-report

NHS Choices

0300 123 1053
www.nhs.uk

If you are a carer, help and support is available from NHS Choices via the Carers Direct Helpline service. You can get advice on your personal support needs and for the person you are caring for. There is information available on assessments, benefits and specialist national and local sources of help and a myriad of other resources available.

Find out more from: *www.nhs.uk/conditions/social-care-and-support-guide/Pages/what-is-social-care.aspx*

Citizens Advice Bureau

0345 404 0506
www.citizensadvice.org.uk

You might have to wait for an appointment but the online resources are excellent.

They are my first point of reference if I'm talking to someone who has any kind of problem and I've had occasion to use them myself. My gran used to volunteer and I've been an advocate ever since.

When you are dog tired, confused, and haven't a clue where to turn, then give them a call. With kindness and understanding they will guide you towards the official bodies from which to get help.

Carers UK

020 7378 4999
www.carersuk.org

You will be guided through a carer's assessment that will determine what help you might qualify for. You may be entitled to help with bills, reduction in fees, prescription costs and much more. Yes, you have to declare earnings and savings which some might object to but in the circumstances I would say get as much help as you can from the beginning. The more help you get, and the sooner you get it, the chances are the more successful you will be.

Help may be as simple as getting someone to sit with your child so you get a break to attend appointments, join a class, or meet with a friend. This is especially important if you are a single parent. We don't all live close to other family members and even if we do they will possibly work and have busy lives themselves. You still need to give yourself a break from the responsibility in order to keep body and soul functioning.

If you are concerned that your adult child is not eating you may be able to receive funds from Carers UK to pay for someone to sit with them while they eat. This might sound extreme but if you need support take advantage of whatever you can because you will burn yourself out much quicker if you try to do everything yourself. You need to retain a life of your own but more importantly you need to keep paying the bills and it won't help you do your job properly if your mind is elsewhere.

Top Five Things to Remember

If you have discovered your child, partner, friend or family member has an eating disorder please:

- Get help fast.
- Make a noise.
- Don't take no for an answer.
- Trust your instincts. Be proactive, don't let it rest. Figure what help you want, be noisy, be heard, it's the squeaky wheel that gets the attention – be the squeaky wheel.
- Most of all – take care of yourself. Put yourself top of the list because you are important too!

The Future

So much is being done to raise an awareness of mental health issues and to take away the stigma associated with them. It's going to be a long process but with the internet and social media making more things accessible we can all find help sooner than we did years ago.

Thanks to organisations like B-eat and ongoing research we may be able to find what triggers eating disorders and how best to deal with them. Until then there is hope, there is always hope.

I cannot thank the parents who responded to my questionnaire enough, most especially for their honesty and openness in sharing their experience. My heart goes out to anyone going through this torment and I hope in some small way that you gain comfort and practical advice from this book.

Book Recommendations

Eating Disorders: Helping Your Child Recover
Edited by Steven Bloomfield
Published: Eating Disorders Association
ISBN: 978-0955177217

Eating Disorders: A Parents' Guide
Racheal Bryant-Waugh and Bryan Lask
Publisher: Routledge 2013
ISBN: 978-0415501569

Skills-based Learning for Caring for a Loved One with an Eating Disorder: The New Maudsley Method
Janet Treasure, Gráinne Smith and Anna Crane
Publisher: Routledge
ISBN: 978-0415431583

Help your Teenager Beat an Eating Disorder
James Lock and Daniel Le Grange PhD
Publisher: Guilford Press
ISBN: 978-1462517480

Becoming John
John Evans
Publisher: Xlibris 2011
ISBN: 978-1462877980

Eating Disorders: The Path to Recovery
Dr Kate Middleton
Publisher: Lion Books
ISBN: 978-0745952789

Boys Get Anorexia Too: Coping with Male Eating Disorders in the Family
Jenny Langley
Publisher: Paul Chapman Publishing
ISBN: 978-1412920223

Hope with Eating Disorders
Lynn Crilly
Publisher: Hay House Insights
ISBN: 978-1848508927

Anorexia and other Eating Disorders: How to Help Your Child Eat Well and Be Well
Eva Musby
Publisher: APRICA
ISBN: 978-0993059803

Codependent No More
Melody Beattie
Publisher: Hazelden Information & Educational Services
ISBN: 978-0894864025

Where Has My Little Girl Gone?
Tanith Carey
Publisher: Lion Books
ISBN: 978-0745955421

I've included my questionnaire to give an insight to the questions I asked parents and carers.

It was not used to find details of the child's illness but to discover the parental experience, reaction and emotional fallout from caring for a child, no matter their age, with an eating disorder. It was not to find numbers, statistics or measurement but to ascertain that my experience was not odd or unusual but in fact a commonality.

The Questionnaire

All information provided will be treated in confidence and remain strictly confidential. All names (if given) will be changed to protect identity and privacy. Your replies will be used for the book and articles to help other families in this position and your privacy will be protected at all times. All data will be stored securely by number only. No identifying details will remain.

1. Your age
2. Child's age when eating disorder discovered
3. Family structure – married/step-parents/single parent. Age of siblings
4. When and how did you find out your child had an eating disorder?
5. What was your initial reaction? How did you feel?
6. Were you aware of things that might have indicated a problem?
7. Did you feel at any time that you were in denial as to what was going on?

8. How did you find out?
9. How long had it been going on for before coming to light?
10. How and when did you tell other family members? How did they react?
11. Did you confide in/talk to anyone else about it? If not, what were the reasons for this?
12. Were you aware of any help available for your child?
13. Where did you find help and support for your child in the first instance?
14. Was the medical profession helpful or did you have to battle for support?
15. Where did you find help and support for yourself? Did you know of any resources for care givers?
16. Did it cause problems within the family? How were relationships affected?
17. How did other members cope? Did they support you?
18. What ongoing support and help was available for your child?
19. What was the worst moment/experience for you?
20. Were there any funny or farcical moments? Sometimes having a sense of humour is the only thing that gets you through.
21. Any ongoing strategies that helped you cope with the situation? Did you come up with these yourself or did you get them from another source, i.e. book, friend, website?

22. What helped most? Talking with friends/family/helplines/online forums/support group?
23. On reflection, what would you do differently (if anything)?
24. Do you have any advice that you would like to pass on that might help others that may find themselves in your situation?

Sometimes when it looks like things are falling apart they are really falling into place.

Acknowledgements

I'd like to thank all those people who supported me on this journey.

To the parents that responded to my questionnaire and the many friends I made at Care Groups, especially Sharon, Lorraine and Carole and the staff at Restored.

To Beat and Kimmeridge Court for putting out requests with reference to the questionnaire through their newsletters, noticeboards and websites.

To Dr Ciarán Newell for his precious time and for the wonderful work he and his team do at Kimmeridge Court – most especially, Kate.

To Judy Hall for her guidance in completing the book – and the Kick Ass. It worked.

Helen Baggott, for her precision, attention to detail and confidence boosts.

My marvellous long-time friend and mentor Margaret Graham who has guided my writing and encouraged me since we first met. She believed in me when I didn't believe in myself.

For my mum, dad and sisters for always being there with love and support. Best cheerleading team ever.

It goes without saying that without the support of my husband, sons and lovely daughters-in-law I wouldn't be standing. Thank you seems too small a word to express all I want to say.

To Luke, for loving my daughter until she learned how to love herself again.

And to my beautiful, strong, brave daughter who fought back. Thank you for the gift and the Mother's Day promise made all those years ago. I admire and love you more than you will ever know.

ABOUT THE AUTHOR

Tracy's articles and short stories have been published all over the world in magazines like *Woman's Weekly, My Weekly, Take A Break, Best* and *The People's Friend.* A regular speaker at writing festivals, she also judges short story competitions and organises creative writing workshops.

She lives in Dorset with her husband and springer spaniel, both of whom are hyperactive and hard work.

For more information about Tracy go to:
www.tracybaines.co.uk

Made in the USA
Charleston, SC
07 March 2017